SECOND EDITION

WORKBOOK

Australia · Brazil · Mexico · Singapore · United Kingdom · United States

Wonderful World 4 Workbook, Second Edition

Vice President, Editorial Director: John McHugh

Executive Editor: Siân Mavor

Commissioning Editor: Kayleigh Buller

Senior Development Editor: Karen Haller Beer

Head of Strategic Marketing EMEA ELT:
 Charlotte Ellis

Product Marketing Executive: Ellen Setterfield

Head of Production and Design: Celia Jones

Content Project Manager: Melissa Beavis

Manufacturing Manager: Eyvett Davis

Art Director: Brenda Carmichael

Cover Design: Lisa Trager

Interior Design and Composition:
 Lumina Datamatics, Inc.

© 2019 National Geographic Learning, a Cengage Learning Company

ALL RIGHTS RESERVED. No part of this work covered by the copyright herein may be reproduced or distributed in any form or by any means, except as permitted by U.S. copyright law, without the prior written permission of the copyright owner.

"National Geographic", "National Geographic Society" and the Yellow Border Design are registered trademarks of the National Geographic Society ® Marcas Registradas

For product information and technology assistance, contact us at
Cengage Learning Customer & Sales Support, cengage.com/contact

For permission to use material from this text or product,
submit all requests online at **cengage.com/permissions**
Further permissions questions can be emailed to
permissionrequest@cengage.com

Workbook: Level 4
ISBN: 978-1-4737-6064-6

National Geographic Learning
Cheriton House, North Way
Andover, Hampshire, SP10 5BE
United Kingdom

National Geographic Learning, a Cengage Learning Company, has a mission to bring the world to the classroom and the classroom to life. With our English language programs, students learn about their world by experiencing it. Through our partnerships with National Geographic and TED Talks, they develop the language and skills they need to be successful global citizens and leaders.

Locate your local office at **international.cengage.com/region**

Visit National Geographic Learning online at **NGL.Cengage.com/ELT**
Visit our corporate website at **www.cengage.com**

Photo Credits

© **Alamy Stock Photo: 20(br)** Reinhard Dirscherl; **76(ml)** Hero Images Inc; **102(bl)** Blickwinkel
© **Dreamstime: 16(ml)** Tomasz Markowski; **22(br)** Fintastique; **38(tl)** Yuri ArcursDreamstime; **38(bl)** Yuri ArcursDreamstime; **38(tr)** Rmarmion; **38(br)** Hongqi Zhang (aka Michael Zhang); **50(tl)** Socrates; **70** Rainer Junker; **94(bm)** Simonkr; **98(tl)** Tom Dowd; **101(bkgd)** Freesurf69; **110(tr)** Alvaro Ennes

© **Fotolia: 20(bm)** Westend61; **44(tl)** PhotoCD; **65** Barbema

© **Getty Images: 18** Richard Nowitz/National Geographic; **32** Richard Nowitz/National Geographic; **39** BananaStock; **44(br)** Xavierarnau/E+; **46** Stephen Alvarez/National Geographic; **56(tl)** Peter M. Fisher/Corbis; **56(tr)** JGI/Tom Grill/Blend Images; **58(tl)** Fuse/Corbis; **60** Paul Nicklen/National Geographic; **74** Scott S. Warren/National Geographic; **76(tl)** Vstock; **76(bl)** Steve Dunwell/Age Fotostock; **82(tm)** Maskot; **82(bm)** Simonkr/ E+; **82(br)** Adamkaz/E+; **88** Richard Nowitz/National Geographic; **100(br)** DEA PICTURE LIBRARY/De Agostini Picture Library; **102(tr)** Paul Zahl/National Geographic; **110(bm)** Jupiterimages/PHOTOS.com; **112(tm)** Jupiterimages/PHOTOS.com; **112(br)** Maskot

© **iStockphoto: 8** Paulbanton; **28(b)** Loooby; **43(bl)** WolfeLarry; **68** Alina555; **76(bm)** RapidEye; **82(tr)** Aleksandar Milutinovic; **100(bm)** Cobalt; **104(bl)** Marcomanzini; **104(br)** Ra3rn; **108(tl)** Enjoylife2; **108(bl)** Kreci; **112(bl)** Simonkr; **112(bm)** Aleksandar Milutinovic

© **Shutterstock: 6** Shutterstock; **7** Ersler Dmitry; **11** Gladskikh Tatiana; **13** Photographee.eu; **14 (b)** Odua Images; **15** Tony Campbell; **16(tl)** Terence Mendoza; **16(bl)** Lana B; **16(tr)** Ingvald Kaldhussater; **16(mr)** Orientaly; **16(br)** Chad McDermott; **16(b)** Elxeneize; **17** Alex Garaev; **20(tl)** Sergey Orlov; **20(tm)** Sk Elena; **20(tr)** Michael Wick; **20(bl)** Alena Ozerova; **22(tl)** Maga; **22(bl)** Jenny Solomon; **22(tm)** 279photo Studio; **22(bm)** Andrey Khrolenok; **22(tr)** Denis Radovanovic; **22(b)** Marcel Jancovic; **24** DaCek; **25(tl)** Elena Elisseeva; **25(bl)** Beaubeau; **28(bl)** Marco Mayer; **28(bml)** Joe Gough; **28(bmr)** Volosina; **28(tm)** Moving Moment; **28(bm)** Kallitu; **28(tr)** Vladis Studio; **28(br)** Peleg Elkalay; **30** Mic Hael; **34(tl)** Sagir; **34(bl)** Africa Studio; **34(tm)** Andrei Kholmov; **34(bm)** Fedorov Oleksiy; **34(tr)** Ase; **34(br)** Lorraine Swanson; **36(t)** Volodymyr Burdiak; **36(b)** Olena Mykhaylova; **43(bm)** Alexandr Shebanov; **43(br)** Shutterstock; **44(bl)** Helder Almeida; **44(tm)** Peter Hansen; **44(bm)** Dmitry Melnikov; **44(tr)** Mike Flippo; **48** Anatoli Styf; **50(bl)** Stephanie Frey; **50(tm)** Danijel Micka; **50(bm)** Hfng; **50(tr)** Eky Studio; **50(br)** Riekephotos; **50(b)** Cozyta; **54** Alvaro German Vilela; **56(bm)** Phanu D Pongvanit; **56tm)** Bunyarit; **56(bm)** Adela Lia Rusu; **56(br)** Yuri Samsonov; **58(tm)** Darren Baker; **56(tr)** Lisa F. Young; **56(bl)** Hurst Photo; **56(bm)** Stenic56; **63** Matty Symons; **64** Serp; **67** Brent Wong; **76(tm)** Bibiphoto; **76(mm)** Monkey Business Images; **76(tr)** Pagina; **76(mr)** Nykonchuk Oleksii; **78** Philip Lange; **82 (tl)** Syda Productions; **82(bl)** Pressmaster; **83(tl)** Liv Friis-Larsen; **83(ml)** Suhendri; **83(bl)** Raisa Kanareva; **83(tr)** Travellight; **83(mr)** Mostovyi Sergii Igorevich; **83(br)** Paul Cowan; **84** T-Design; **87** ArtFamily; **90(tl)** Galina Barskaya; **90(bl)** Halfpoint; **90(tr)** AVAVA; **90(br)** Denis Radovanovic; **91** Marcin Balcerzak; **92(tl)** PhotoBeard; **92(bl)** Alon Othnay; **92(tr)** Terence Mendoza; **92(br)** Lana B; **94(tl)** Pryzmat; **94(bl)** Anita Colic; **94(tm)** Jan Kranendonk; **94(tr)** Kristian Sekulic; **94(br)** Glenda; **95** Joggie Botma; **96(t)** Mindy W.M.Chung; **96(mt)** Lim Yong Hian; **96(mb)** CKP1001; **96(b)** Bonchan; **98(bl)** Monkey Business Images; **98(tm)** Africa Studio; **98(bm)** Picsfive; **98(tr)** AVAVA; **98(br)** Mark Graves; **99(t)** Chippix; **99(b)** Monkey Business Images; **100(tl)** Sculpies; **100(tl)** Scott Rothstein; **100(tm)** JoLin; **100 (tr)** Totophotos; **101(tl)** Leoks; **101(tr)** SueC; **102(tl)** A9photo; **102(br)** Chai Kian Shin; **104(tl)** Amy Walters; **104(bm)** Yuri Samsonov; **104(tm)** StudioNewmarket; **104(tr)** GeorgeAA; **106(tl)** Jan Kranendonk; **106(bl)** Joe Gough; **106(tm)** Francisco Orellana; **106(bm)** Newphotoservice; **106(tr)** Werayuth Tes; **106(br)** Stefan Ataman; **108(tl)** Neale Cousland; **108(br)** Ssuaphotos; **110(tl)** Chris Jenner; **110(bl)** JCVStock; **110(tm)** Tom Nance; **110(br)** Pagina; **112(tl)** Kurhan; **112(tr)** Pcruciatti

Printed in the United Kingdom by CPI Antony Rowe
Print Number: 08   Print Year: 2023

Contents

	Page
Unit 0: Introduction	4
Unit 1: Being Together	6
Unit 2: Where Do You Live?	12
Review 1: Units 1–2	18
Unit 3: Try Something New	20
Unit 4: Food and Drink	26
Review 2: Units 3–4	32
Unit 5: Education	34
Unit 6: Our Amazing Bodies	40
Review 3: Units 5–6	46
Unit 7: All Around Us	48
Unit 8: Protecting the Planet	54
Review 4: Units 7–8	60
Unit 9: City Life	62
Unit 10: Share and Enjoy	68
Review 5: Units 9–10	74
Unit 11: From Here to There	76
Unit 12: Jobs	82
Review 6: Units 11–12	88
Projects: 1–12	90

Introduction

Numbers to 100,000

1 Write the words.

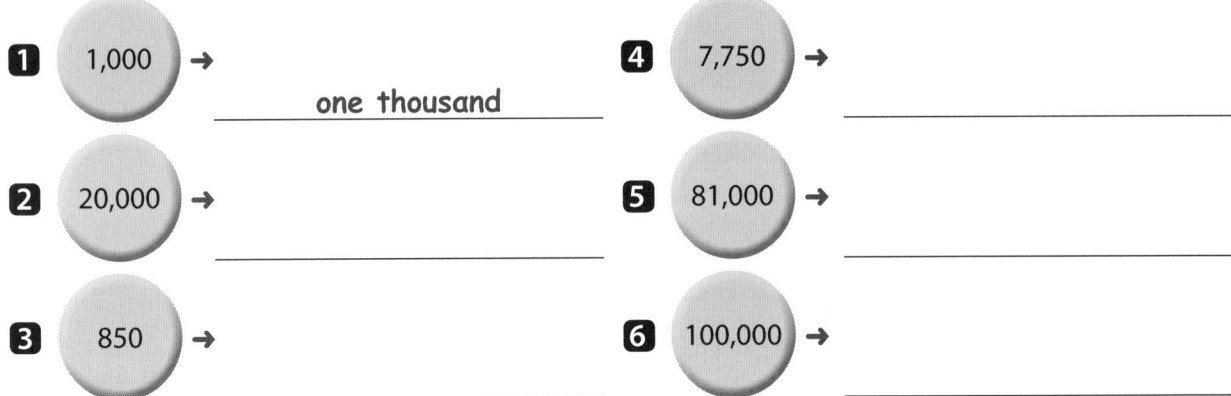

1. 1,000 → one thousand
2. 20,000 → _____
3. 850 → _____
4. 7,750 → _____
5. 81,000 → _____
6. 100,000 → _____

Years and dates

2 Match.

1. 1820
2. 1460
3. 2020
4. 1701
5. 1979

a. fifteenth century
b. twentieth century
c. nineteenth century
d. eighteenth century
e. twenty-first century

Subject and object pronouns

3 Circle the correct words.

1. This is Karen's pencil. She bought **it** / **him** this morning.
2. There are Jim and Louise. Let's go and play with **us** / **them**.
3. I'm writing to my aunt. I write to **him** / **her** every week.
4. We're hiding. Can you see **us** / **it**?
5. Please don't shout. I can hear **them** / **you**.
6. This is Peter's pizza. It's for **him** / **me**.

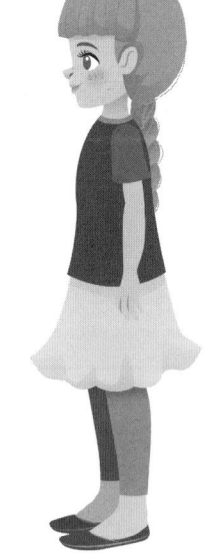

Possessive pronouns

4 Complete the sentences with these words.

| her | its | ~~my~~ | our | their | your |

1. I'm thirteen and **my** sister is ten.
2. We have got a big bedroom with all _____ toys in it.
3. Carla and Ryan are staying with _____ grandmother this weekend.
4. I can't believe Marie is _____ sister. She doesn't look like you.
5. The dog is looking for _____ bone.
6. This is Sarah's present. It's for _____ .

4 UNIT 0

There is / are / was / were

5 Write the correct form of *there is, there are, there was* or *there were*.

1 ___Is there___ a dolphin in the water?

2 Look! _____ a car in the park.

3 _____ any horses at the farm yesterday.

4 I'm sorry, but _____ any books for you today.

5 No, _____ a phone in the house.

6 _____ a big swimming pool at our hotel last summer.

Prepositions of place

6 Complete the pictures with these words.

under   behind   between   next to   in front of   ~~on~~

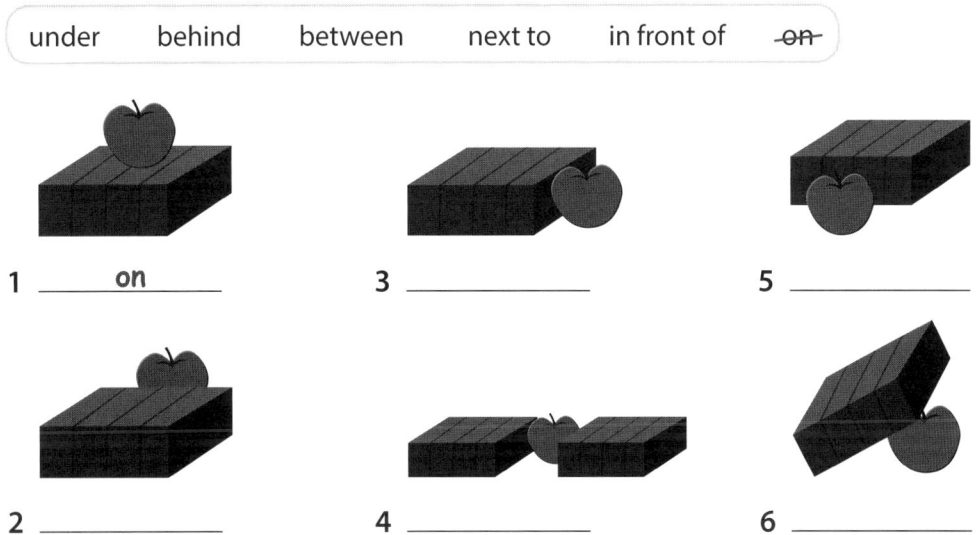

1 ___on___   3 _____   5 _____

2 _____   4 _____   6 _____

Question words

7 Answer the questions.

1 What year were you born? _____

2 Where do you live? _____

3 How do you get to school? _____

4 Who is your favourite singer? _____

5 When do you go to bed? _____

6 Whose pen are you using to write this? _____

1 Being Together

Lesson 1

1 Circle the correct words.

1. I love comedies. They make me **laugh** / **lazy**.
2. My grandma has five **grandchildren** / **child**.
3. My cousin is very **clever** / **lazy**. He's always in bed.
4. I'm an only **niece** / **child**. I don't have brothers or sisters.
5. 'Do you **laugh** / **enjoy** swimming?' 'Yes, I do.'
6. My **nephew** / **niece** is very kind. He's a nurse.

2 Circle the odd one out.

1. niece   nephew   (only child)
2. grandparent   sister   week
3. huge   lazy   naughty
4. laugh   smell   enjoy
5. aunt   uncle   grandparent

3 Match.

1. Where's Alex?   a Thanks.
2. Thank you for the invitation.   b He's never on time.
3. I haven't got time to talk now.   c It's my pleasure.
4. Look at the time!   d OK, I won't waste your time.
5. Have a great time at the park.   e We're going to be late!

6 UNIT 1

4 Complete with the present simple of the verbs in brackets.

1 This flower ___smells___ (smell) nice!
2 _____ you _____ (enjoy) working at the harbour?
3 Robbie _____ (not look) excited.
4 I _____ (not laugh) at the teacher's jokes.
5 _____ they _____ (go) to the island every year?
6 Grandpa _____ (know) a lot of interesting stories.
7 _____ he _____ (swim) in the sea in the winter?
8 Those lazy people always _____ (waste) our time.

5 Choose the correct answers.

1 Do they _____ here?
  a) live
  b) lives
  c) doesn't live

2 Clare _____ their company.
  a enjoy
  b enjoys
  c don't enjoy

3 'Do you always have a good time here?' 'Yes, _____.'
  a they do
  b we do
  c she does

4 I _____ at the swimming pool.
  a works
  b doesn't work
  c don't work

5 She _____ like people who waste time.
  a doesn't
  b not
  c don't

6 Does it usually _____ on Cortuga Island in spring?
  a don't rain
  b rains
  c rain

6 Put the adverbs of frequency in brackets in the correct place.

1 Grandma helps me with my homework. (usually)
   Grandma usually helps me with my homework.
2 The three o'clock train is late. (never)
   _____
3 We don't watch TV in our house. (often)
   _____
4 Mum works on Saturdays. (usually)
   _____
5 Sam goes swimming in the morning. (sometimes)
   _____
6 My friends are on time. (always)
   _____

Lesson 2

1 Complete the sentences with these words.

~~population~~   hurt   protect   hunt   danger

1 The __population__ of our town is 40,000.

2 Lions are good fathers. They always _____ their cubs.

3 Leopards often _____ at night.

4 We mustn't _____ wild animals.

5 Big cats, like cheetahs, are in _____ .

2 Complete the crossword puzzle.

Across
1 A l__eopard__ is a big cat with spots.
6 The p_____ is the number of people in a town or country.
7 Lions h_____ when they need food.

Down
2 Farmers want to p_____ their animals from big cats.
3 The s_____ is yellow. You can see it in the sky.
4 Many animals in the world are in d_____.
5 A g_____ is an animal with a very long neck.

3 Circle the correct words.

1 Lions take **care** / **after** of their cubs.

2 I'm not **frightened** / **favourite** of the leopard.

3 The Jouberts' work **reaches** / **cares** millions of people.

4 Farmers are **finding** / **killing** the big cats that eat their animals.

5 People must **look after** / **in fact** animals that are in danger.

6 My shoes are old. **In fact** / **Usually**, I'm buying new ones today.

8 UNIT 1

4 Complete the sentences with the present continuous of these verbs. Use the affirmative or negative form.

> drink   fight   ~~hunt~~   play   protect   visit

1 The giraffes <u>aren't hunting</u> for food. ✗
2 We _____ with our toys. ✓
3 I _____ my grandmother at the weekend. ✗
4 The father _____ the baby lions. ✓
5 You _____ my orange juice! ✓
6 Jenny and her brother are happy and they _____ . ✗

5 Put the words in the correct order.

1 going / the group / at the moment / is / home
<u>The group is going home at the moment.</u>
2 isn't / her food / today / eating / Jan
_____
3 ? / are / a film / watching / now / the viewers
_____
4 ? / I / hurting / the bird / am
_____
5 having fun / this morning / aren't / you
_____
6 are / tomorrow / we / the baby / looking after
_____

6 Look at the pictures and write questions and short answers with the present continuous.

1 the lion / sleep / on the grass
<u>Is the lion sleeping on the grass?</u>
<u>Yes, it is.</u>

2 Mark and Anna / have fun
_____

3 the grandmother / look after / the baby
_____

4 the people / run away
_____

5 we / take care of / the lion
_____

6 the boy / watch / a TV show
_____

9

Lesson 3

1 **Complete with these words.**

| carrot | football | friend | horse | ~~lesson~~ | party |

1 What time is your piano ___lesson___ ?

2 Can you come to my _____ on Saturday?

3 My dad's watching _____ on TV again!

4 Jane is Sally's best _____ and they do a lot of fun things together.

5 This _____ wins all the races.

6 My pet rabbit eats a _____ every day.

2 **Choose the correct answers.**

1 They are going on holiday _____ .
  a never
  b usually
  c (tomorrow)

2 They're _____ TV at the moment.
  a watching
  b are watching
  c watch

3 We _____ the horses water every day.
  a is giving
  b are giving
  c give

4 She always _____ at my jokes.
  a is laughing
  b laughs
  c aren't laughing

5 I _____ understand this word.
  a doesn't
  b don't
  c am not

6 We _____ go swimming.
  a often
  b once a week
  c tomorrow

7 We _____ with our cousins next month.
  a don't stay
  b aren't staying
  c stay

8 Look! That kitten _____ .
  a runs
  b are running
  c is running

3 **Match.**

SAY IT LIKE THIS!

1 He always talks to me. — b
2 Look at my new bike.
3 Lara's watching TV again.
4 Look at that lion!
5 My sister is very good at football.
6 Max, the cat, eats lots of food.

a She's so lazy!
b He's so nice!
c It's so cool!
d It's so frightening!
e He's so fat!
f She's so fast!

10 UNIT 1

4 Read the description of Karen's family and circle the correct words.

Hello, my name's Karen and this is my family.

I'm 12 years old and I have got two brothers and a sister. I love music! I (1) **now / usually** go to piano lessons (2) **this morning / at the weekends**. But (3) **this / every** weekend we are going on holiday to Egypt. Our friends live there!

My friends, Gamal and Amani, are great fun. They (4) **today / always** make me laugh. We love the sea, so we (5) **never / sometimes** go to the beach.

My mum and dad love Egypt, too. They take us there (6) **every summer / at the moment**.

We've also got a pet lizard called Jason, but you can't see him in this photo! He's very shy!

Remember!

We use these adverbs of frequency with the present simple: **always, usually, often, sometimes, never.**

We use these time expressions with the present simple: **every day / week / weekend / spring / summer / autumn / winter, once a week / month / year, at the weekends.**

We use these time expressions with the present continuous: **this morning / spring / summer / autumn / winter, next week / month / year, now, at the moment, today, tomorrow.**

5 Write a description of your friend's family. Use this plan to help you.

Paragraph 1: Write something about your best friend.
Paragraph 2: Write about your friend's brother(s) or sister(s) (**or** his / her aunt / uncle / cousin, etc.).
Paragraph 3: Write about your friend's parents.
Paragraph 4: Write about your friend's pet.

2 Where Do You Live?

Lesson 1

1 Find the house-related words and use them to complete the sentences.

1 Our new _____oven_____ cooks food very well.
2 Please close the _____. I'm cold!
3 Our _____ has a lot of food inside.
4 I'm in the _____ and the water is cold.
5 This is grandpa's favourite _____.
6 Wash your hands after you use the _____.
7 Your white shirt is in your _____.
8 The girls sat on the _____.

2 Look at the pictures and write the correct phrases.

Be careful, Maged!   I'm coming.   Nice to meet you.   See you later!   ~~Waiter! Waiter!~~

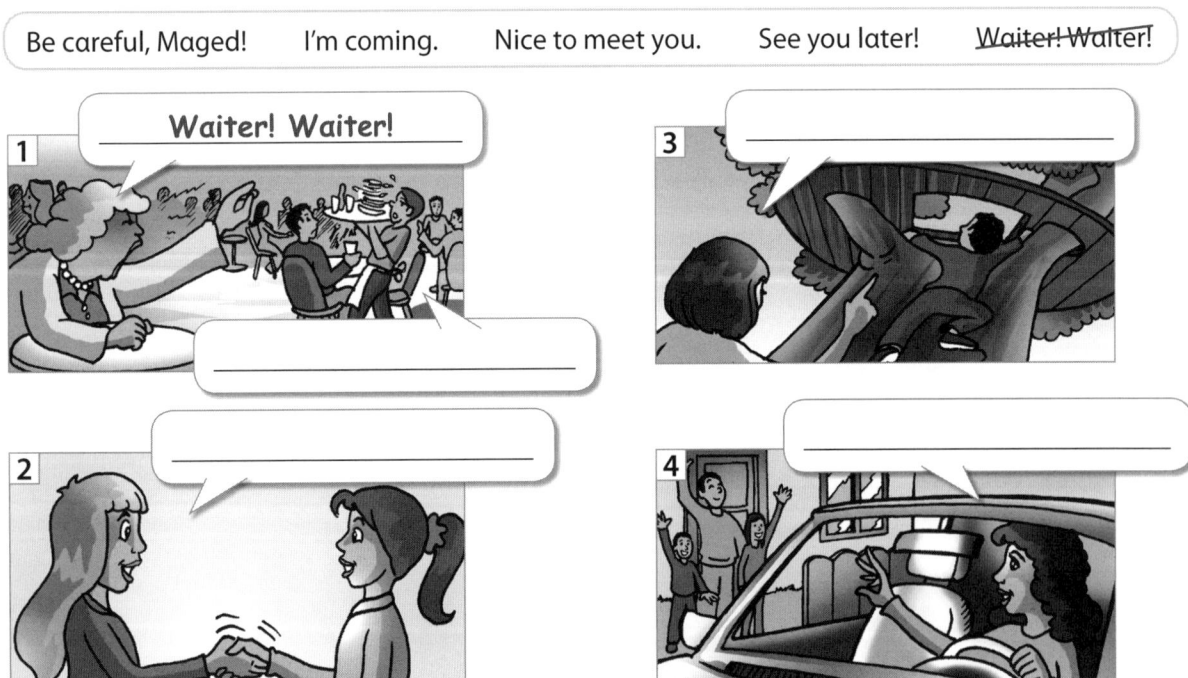

3 Circle the correct words.

1 I like your new coffee **table** / **oven**!
2 Can you **save** / **pay** for the cake? I don't have any money.
3 Ben **hated** / **saved** his money for a guitar.
4 Please put your dirty cups in the **oven** / **sink**.
5 I hated my old room. It was **awful** / **rich**!
6 We aren't **rich** / **careful**, but we have a nice house.

4 Complete the dialogue with the past simple of the verbs in brackets.

Jade: Wow, your new room is amazing!
Alek: I know. I (1) __finished__ (finish) it last week.
I (2) _____ (want) a cool room and now I've got it.
Jade: You've got so many cool things in it.
Alek: Yes, I (3) _____ (plan) it for a long time.
Jade: Black and white are cool colours! And it's so tidy.
Alek: We (4) _____ (tidy) it this morning. Oh, and my older sister (5) _____ (help) too. I love my new room!

5 Rewrite the sentences in the negative form of the past simple.

1 We arrived at five o'clock.
We didn't arrive at five o'clock.

2 They looked at a new wardrobe yesterday.
_____

3 She wanted a coffee.
_____

4 I moved here last year.
_____

5 He followed that man.
_____

6 The waiter opened the fridge.
_____

7 It rained all last week.
_____

8 Ben stayed with his aunt last summer.
_____

6 Look at the pictures and write questions and short answers with the past simple.

1 Maria / watch / TV / last night
Did Maria watch TV last night?
No, she didn't.

2 the cat / like / the new rug
_____

3 Chris and Steve / play / the piano
_____

4 they / clean / the kitchen
_____

5 Tim / stay / at home / yesterday
_____

6 the Parkers / arrive at the party / at nine o'clock
_____

Lesson 2

1 Circle the odd one out.

1 rug	floor	(washing machine)
2 rubbish	balcony	roof
3 modern	poor	rich
4 vacuum cleaner	garden	microwave oven
5 plastic	glass	bookcase
6 earthquake	furniture	bedroom

2 Circle the correct words.

1 The teacher put the book in the **bookcase** / **shower**.

2 Let's have lunch on the **bedroom** / **balcony**.

3 Mr Ingenieri made his house from **modern** / **glass** bottles.

4 I **reuse** / **make** plastic bottles by making furniture out of them.

5 There's lots of **rugs** / **rubbish** in your bedroom. Please tidy it!

6 Potatoes cook quickly in a **fridge** / **microwave oven**.

3 Complete the paragraph with these words.

> glass   rich   modern   washing machine   rubbish   ~~earthquake~~

Ron's family lost their home when an (1) __earthquake__ hit in 2011. Life was hard. They didn't have the money to buy a new house, because they weren't very (2) _____ . But Ron's mum had an idea. '(3) _____ doesn't cost any money, so let's build a house out of it!' she said.

The family talked to a house designer and soon they started building their new house. They used old (4) _____ bottles for the walls and old plastic bottles for the roof. They used hundreds of plastic bags for the floor. Ron helped his parents make the house.

Now, Ron and his family live in their new house. They have a (5) _____ to wash their clothes, an oven to cook their food and a nice, (6) _____ bathroom. It's just like other houses, but it's made from old bottles!

4 Complete the sentences with the past simple of the verbs in brackets.

1. Mark _____put_____ (put) the rubbish in the bin.
2. Darren and George _____ (make) a cake this morning.
3. We _____ (sit) on the balcony last night.
4. The children _____ (eat) lunch at home.
5. She _____ (draw) a picture of her bedroom.
6. They _____ (see) an elephant in the street!

5 Complete the sentences with the past simple of these verbs.

| become | come | ~~give~~ | go | grow | lose | sell | tell |

1. My parents _____gave_____ my aunt their old washing machine.
2. John was sick, so he _____ to the hospital.
3. Dina and Lisa met in Alexandria and they _____ best friends.
4. Debbie _____ me that she was having a party.
5. He _____ his book yesterday. He doesn't know where it is.
6. My grandmother _____ from a small village in France.
7. They _____ their house and moved to another town.
8. Kevin _____ up in Maryhill.

6 Write sentences in the past simple.

1. Sally / catch / the ball
   Sally caught the ball.
2. Donald / buy / a vacuum cleaner
   _____
3. the kitten / find / a ball
   _____
4. Mum and Dad / get sick
   _____
5. I / meet / my friends
   _____
6. Grandpa / take / a taxi
   _____

Lesson 3

1 Match.

1 sitting room d
2 dining room ☐
3 houseboat ☐
4 bathroom ☐
5 garden ☐
6 cottage ☐

2 Make a list of the furniture in your bedroom.

3 Tell your partner about your bedroom.

4 Complete the dialogue with these words.

SAY IT LIKE THIS!

cottage   flat   is   ~~live~~   move

Eric: Where do you (1) ___live___, Danny?

Danny: I live in a huge (2) _____ in the city centre.

Eric: Cool! You're near all the shops and cafés.

Danny: That's right. I love it there. I lived in an old (3) _____ in a small village before. It was really boring.

Eric: When did you (4) _____ in?

Danny: I moved into the flat a year ago.

Eric: (5) _____ the flat modern?

Danny: Yes, it's very modern. Why don't you come at the weekend?

16 UNIT 2

5 Circle the correct words.

HOUSEBOAT TO RENT!

This beautiful houseboat is on the river (1) **so** / **because** it has got a nice view. It's a great home for young people. It's got four bedrooms (2) **and** / **but** a big sitting room. You can cook all your meals here (3) **so** / **because** there's a modern kitchen. It hasn't got a dining room (4) **and** / **but** there is a big table in the kitchen. The houseboat isn't new (5) **but** / **and** the furniture is. You can live in this houseboat (6) **but** / **and** enjoy the river too!

> **Remember!**
>
> Linking words make our writing better:
> - **and** adds something else to a sentence
> - **but** shows that something is different to another thing
> - **because** gives the reason for something
> - **so** gives the result of something.
>
> The flat is big **and** modern.
>
> The house is beautiful **but** old.
>
> I changed schools **because** I moved house.
>
> They live in London **so** they speak English.

6 Write an advert for a house. Use this plan to help you.

Answer the questions:

What kind of house is it?

Where is it?

Who can live there?

How many rooms are there? What are they?

Is the house old or new?

Is the furniture modern / comfortable / old?

What can you do there?

Review 1 — Units 1–2

1 Read the text about a house in Barcelona.

Barcelona has got many beautiful buildings. The Casa Batlló, a house at 43 Passeig de Gràcia, is one of them.

The house belonged to Josep Batlló and he lived there with his family. All the families on the Passeig de Gràcia wanted to have beautiful houses. Batlló wanted his old house to look more modern. Antoni Gaudi and Josep Maria Jujol did the job. They began work on the house in 1904.

Gaudi and Jujol changed many things. The house is famous today because of its front. It has got many different shapes and colours and it has also got incredible balconies. The roof is also very special because it looks like a dragon's back.

Are you a fan of unusual houses? Then visit the Casa Batlló and the other fantastic buildings on Barcelona's Passeig de Gràcia.

2 Answer the questions.

1. Where did Josep Batlló live? <u>at 43 Passeig de Gràcia (in Barcelona)</u>
2. Who did he live with?
3. Who wanted to have beautiful houses?
4. When did Gaudi and Jujol begin work on the Casa Batlló?
5. What has the front of the Casa Batlló got?

3 Choose the correct answers.

1 ____ at the time! Let's go home.
   a Waste   (b) Look   c Be

2 I really ____ Grandma's birthday party this year.
   a laughed   b enjoyed
   c looked after

3 Lionesses always take care ____ their cubs.
   a of   b for   c after

4 Our visit to the town was ____.
   a only   b rude   c awful

5 Please be ____ with the baby!
   a hurt   b careful   c protect

6 Joe looks sad, but ____ fact he's happy.
   a for   b on   c in

7 We always put milk in the ____.
   a shower   b oven   c fridge

8 I love looking out of the ____.
   a window   b balcony   c roof

9 Put your dirty clothes in the ____.
   a microwave oven   b vacuum cleaner
   c washing machine

10 Jan's flat is very ____.
   a modern   b lucky   c mean

11 They've got a new ____ for their bedroom floor.
   a sink   b sofa   c rug

12 Let's ____ that old, glass bottle.
   a reuse   b rubbish   c pay

4 Choose the correct answers.

1 Kate ____ at the weekends.
   a works always   b always work
   (c) always works

2 ____ after the children in the evenings?
   a She looks   b Does she look
   c She doesn't

3 'Does it snow here in winter?' 'Yes, ____.'
   a it snows   b it does   c it doesn't

4 Look! Those lions ____ on the grass.
   a fight   b is fighting
   c are fighting

5 'Is your dad sleeping at the moment?' 'No, ____.'
   a he doesn't   b he isn't sleep
   c he isn't

6 What are you doing ____?
   a tomorrow   b at the weekends
   c every day

7 They always ____ TV after dinner.
   a are watching   b watch
   c watching

8 ____ Sam love football?
   a Is   b Do   c Does

9 Did you ____ your bedroom last night?
   a tidied   b tidies   c tidy

10 They ____ arrive on time.
   a didn't   b not   c wasn't

11 Donna ____ a new bookcase last week.
   a bought   b buys   c is buying

12 Did he ____ the boy some biscuits?
   a gave   b give   c gives

3 Try Something New

Lesson 1

1 Match.

1. equipment — e
2. explore
3. dive
4. hobby
5. deep

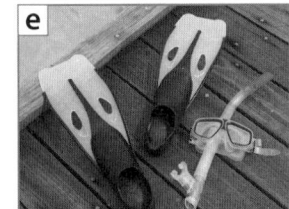

2 Circle the correct words.

1. Why don't you take **up** / on tennis?
2. Let's try **in** / **out** bungee jumping.
3. Can you please **turn** / **give** on the light?
4. Careful! Don't use **up** / **on** all the air in the tank.
5. Don't **try** / **give** up, Paul. Try again!
6. I ended **up** / **in** staying at home last night.

3 Complete the dialogue with these words.

| scuba diving   sure   explore   equipment   ~~hobby~~   wrong |

Sam: Let's try a new (1) ___hobby___, Jamila!

Jamila: OK, what do you want to try?

Sam: How about (2) _____ ?

Jamila: I'm not (3) _____ scuba diving is safe.

Sam: Well, we can learn what to do if something goes (4) _____ .

Jamila: Yes, let's go on a training course!

Sam: Look, there's one here we can do. You learn what (5) _____ you need and how to stay safe.

Jamila: Great! Let's do it. Then we can (6) _____ the sea together.

4 Look at the pictures and write questions and short answers with the past continuous.

1 Sam / watch TV / last night
Was Sam watching TV last night? No, he wasn't.

2 Tom / paint a picture / this morning
_____
_____

3 the girls / have lunch / yesterday at 12.30
_____
_____

4 George / swimming / at this time yesterday
_____
_____

5 they / eat lunch / in their kitchen / on Sunday
_____
_____

6 Sarah / study / between five and eight o'clock
_____
_____

5 Choose the correct answers.

1 We were climbing the mountain at _____ .
   a all day
   b four o'clock
   c this time

2 Were _____ football last night?
   a they playing
   b they play
   c playing

3 What were you doing _____ two and five o'clock yesterday?
   a at
   b between
   c on

4 She _____ to her new CD.
   a were listening
   b listening
   c was listening

5 I _____ on the sofa all day yesterday.
   a wasn't lying
   b weren't lying
   c not lie

6 Put the words in the correct order.

1 were / we / at / six / Saturday / reading / o'clock / last
We were reading at six o'clock last Saturday.

2 o'clock / eight / between / and / baby / was / ten / the / crying
_____
_____

3 it / day / yesterday / snowing / was / all
_____
_____

4 we / sending / night / last / were / emails
_____
_____

5 you / last / living / in / year / village / weren't / this / ?
_____
_____

6 trying / my / out / skateboard / my / dad / this / was / morning
_____
_____

Lesson 2

1 Match.

1 trick   d
2 rope   ☐
3 slide ☐
4 hill   ☐
5 pull   ☐
6 tired ☐

a

c

e

b

d

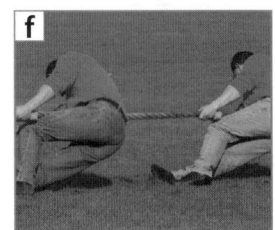
f

2 Complete the advert with these words.

> showing   air   tricks   ~~hill~~   hobby
> snowboards

Come snowboarding!

Do you want to slide down a (1) __hill__ at very fast speeds and maybe even fly through the (2) _____?

You do? Then get on one of our (3) _____ . You can learn to do cool (4) _____ . You'll have a wonderful day!

And soon you'll be (5) _____ off your new tricks to your friends.

Snowboarding is a great (6) _____ !

Call 208 345 9674

3 Circle the correct words.

1 Snowboarding is very **exciting** / excited.
2 Skiing for ten hours is very **tiring** / **tired**.
3 I feel so **relaxing** / **relaxed** after a holiday.
4 Homework is usually **boring** / **bored**.
5 We're really **exciting** / **excited** because we're going horse riding tomorrow.
6 I'm not **interesting** / **interested** in sport.
7 Taking a swim is quite **relaxing** / **relaxed**.
8 I'm going to bed because I'm really **tiring** / **tired**.
9 This film is **interesting** / **interested**. Come and watch it.
10 I'm **boring** / **bored**. Let's go out.

4 Complete the sentences with the past simple or the past continuous of the verbs in brackets.

1. I was skiing when I _____had_____ (have) an accident.
2. They _____ (not go) for a walk while the sun was shining.
3. Ron _____ (play) golf when the rain started.
4. Mandy _____ (not show off) when the teacher walked into the room.
5. The boat _____ (sail) very quickly when the boy fell into the water.
6. Mum _____ (take) my photo while I was sliding down the hill.

5 Look at the pictures and write sentences with the past simple and the past continuous.

1. I / sitting / on the beach / when / the umbrella / fall on me
   I was sitting on the beach when the umbrella fell on me.

2. they / not ice-skate / when / the dog / run onto the ice

3. Dad / bring the boys / cake / while / they / watch TV

4. everyone / have fun / when / Mike / arrive

5. they / eat breakfast / when / the phone ring

6. Laura / hurt / her leg / while / she / play tennis

6 Put the words in the correct order.

1. ? / Grandma / fall / snowboard / she / did / off / snowboarding / while / the / was
   Did Grandma fall off the snowboard while she was snowboarding?

2. were / they / playing / Dad / home / when / football / came / ?

3. ? / make / the twins / while / cake / sleeping / a / were / Mum / did

4. was / in / Joan / the / sitting / garden / the / phone / when / rang / ?

5. ? / accident / showing / the / when / off / were / they / happened

Lesson 3

1 Complete the sentences with these words.

> days   life   like   ~~play~~   time   watch

1 My brothers ___play___ football in the park every Sunday.
2 I don't _____ staying at home at the weekends.
3 I never _____ TV in the evenings.
4 I don't have time for my friends these _____ .
5 What do you do in your free _____ ?
6 I don't like doing homework every night but that's _____ .

2 Circle the correct words.

1 Mara **used** / **use** to go ice-skating every Saturday.
2 Did you **used** / **use** to play the guitar?
3 Jake used to **swimming** / **swim** in the sea.
4 'Did you use to collect stamps?' 'Yes, I **used** / **did**.'
5 She didn't **used** / **use** to like going to the park.
6 'Did Grandpa use to have a TV when he was young?' 'No, he **didn't** / **hadn't**.'

3 Complete the dialogue with these sentences.

SAY IT LIKE THIS!

> Do you like painting?
> Do you like watching TV?
> I hate doing homework.
> Well, I have more time at the weekends.
> ~~What do you do in your free time?~~
> When did you start horse riding?

Interviewer: On today's show, we're talking to young people about their free time. First, we're talking to Jan. She's 16 and she lives in London. Welcome to the show, Jan. (1) ___What do you do in your free time?___

Jan: Well, I haven't got much free time because we get a lot of homework at our school. (2) _____

Interviewer: But you must have some hobbies. (3) _____

Jan: No, I hate painting and drawing. I'm not very good at art.

Interviewer: OK. (4) _____

Jan: No, I can't stand TV. TV shows are really stupid.

Interviewer: What about at the weekends? What do you do then?

Jan: (5) _____ I usually go horse riding.

Interviewer: (6) _____

Jan: I started riding when I was 11.

Interviewer: Thank you, Jan. And now let's talk to Ben. He's 15 and …

4 Complete the story with *and*, *when* or *while*.

Remember!

We use past continuous + past continuous to set the scene for a story. We use **and** to join the two parts of the sentence.

The children were playing a board game **and** their parents were watching television.

We can use past simple + past continuous to talk about things that happen in a story. We use **when** before past simple and **while** before past continuous.

I was running in the park **when** I fell.
I fell **while** I was running in the park.

A dangerous game

Last week I was walking to the swimming pool with my friends (1) __and__ we were talking about our plans for the summer. My best friend Cathy told us about her holiday in Italy last year.

One day, she was walking on the beach (2) _____ a big group of Italian children arrived. They were playing in the water (3) _____ having fun. They were diving from the rocks (4) _____ they were laughing a lot. Then one of the girls dived into the water (5) _____ a boat was passing. The other children shouted her name and jumped into the water. All of the children were looking for her (6) _____ they finally saw her come out of the water. Luckily, she was fine, but she was very scared.

Later the girl spoke to Cathy (7) _____ she was reading her book on the beach. She told Cathy her name was Laura. They talked all afternoon (8) _____ Laura's friends were playing in the sea. They became very good friends. They spent the rest of their holiday together.

5 Write a story about a dangerous game or hobby. Use this plan to help you.

Paragraph 1
Set the scene. Say when and where the dangerous game / hobby happened.

Paragraph 2
Say something about the dangerous game / hobby.

Paragraph 3
Say what happened after the dangerous game / hobby.

4 Food and Drink

Lesson 1

1 Complete the dialogue with these phrases.

> don't believe it   hang on   have got no idea   have a snack   ~~hurry up~~

Annita: Katie! There's a snake in the water!
Katie: What? Where? I have to get out now!
Annita: (1) _Hurry up_! Swim faster! Here, take my hand.
(2) _____, Katie.
Katie: I'm scared! I (3) _____ how the snake got in the water.
Annita: Let's get you out of the water. The snake is getting closer …

Katie: Phew! Thanks for your help, Annita. Where is the snake now?
Annita: I can't see it. I (4) _____! It wasn't a snake, it was my scarf!
Katie: Oh. How silly we are! I'm really hungry now.
Annita: Me too. Being scared makes me hungry. Let's (5) _____!

2 Circle the correct words.

1 Hurry **up** / **on**. I can't wait.
2 Wow, I don't **believe** / **find** it!
3 Hang **up** / **on**! I'm brushing my teeth.
4 'What is it?' 'I've got no **idea** / **thing**.'
5 'I didn't have lunch.' 'Let's **have** / **smell** a snack.'
6 The meal cost 20 Euros **altogether** / **full**.

3 Look at the pictures and write the correct phrases.

> ~~Have a snack.~~   I'm full.   I'm hungry.   I'm thirsty.   It's delicious.   It's disgusting.

26 UNIT 4

4 Complete the sentences with *many*, *much*, *how many* or *how much*.

1 We haven't got _____many_____ tortillas. There are only two.
2 _____ animals are in the van?
3 '_____ is that cake?' 'It's ten pounds.'
4 There isn't _____ water in this glass.
5 Are there _____ bottles of milk in the fridge?
6 _____ butter do I need?
7 There are _____ sweets on the table.
8 Hurry! We haven't got _____ time!

5 Look at the pictures and write *T* for (True) or *F* for (False).

1 There are a lot of children at the picnic. T
2 There are a few chairs in the van.
3 We're buying a little bit of orange juice.
4 There are lots of fish in the bowl.
5 He's giving her a few biscuits.
6 Heather has got a little money.

6 Match.

1 We haven't got much   a are the eggs?
2 How much   b altogether?
3 Grant had a   c chips.
4 How much is it   d lot of sandwiches.
5 You can't have many   e milk. Let's buy some.
6 Can I eat a   f few strawberries?

1 Match.

1 sauce — c
2 pot —
3 meat —
4 raw —
5 seafood —
6 soup —

a
c
e
b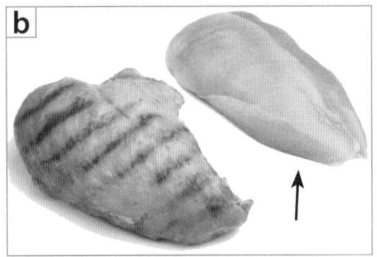
d
f

2 Find the food-related words and use them to complete the sentences.

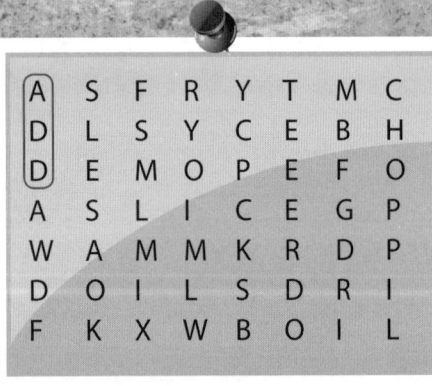

1 __Add__ the cheese to the spaghetti.
2 _____ the chicken for 30 minutes.
3 _____ the onions into little pieces.
4 _____ the tomatoes in the oil.
5 _____ all the ingredients together.
6 _____ the mushrooms and place them on the plate.

3 Circle the odd one out.

1 popcorn — flour — (pot)
2 land — raw — cooked
3 meat — fish — fried
4 oil — water — mix
5 fry — boil — healthy

28 UNIT 4

4 Circle the correct words.

1 Have you got **any** / **some** fried rice?
2 Are there **any** / **some** boiled eggs?
3 There is **every** / **no** sugar in my coffee.
4 I went to **every** / **some** market in town at the weekend!
5 **Every** / **Any** waiter was working yesterday.
6 There aren't **some** / **any** restaurants open today.
7 Here are **some** / **any** carrots for you.
8 Oh, no! There are **any** / **no** vegetables in the fridge.

5 Look at the pictures and complete the sentences with these words.

anybody   anywhere   ~~everywhere~~   nothing   somebody   something

1 Chris looked _everywhere_ for some sweets.
3 There's _____ for lunch.
5 There's _____ at the window.

2 There isn't _____ at the market.
4 Samantha is putting _____ in her mum's food.
6 You can sit _____ you like.

6 Complete the sentences with these words.

any   anything   everybody   everything   no   nowhere   some   ~~someone~~

1 There's _someone_ at the door. Can you open it?
2 Have we got _____ juice?
3 Can I have _____ cold water, please?
4 There's _____ nice for a picnic. Let's eat at home.
5 I can't eat _____ in this restaurant. It only sells fried food!
6 There is _____ milk in the fridge. Please buy some.
7 I really enjoyed the party. _____ was great.
8 _____ is here. Let's eat!

Lesson 3

1 Write the missing letters.

1. You make hot chocolate with this. c <u>o c o a</u> p <u>o w d e r</u>
2. You read this when you are cooking. r _ _ _ _ _
3. You do this to make food warm. h _ _ _
4. You put food in this to cook it. p _ _
5. This is when you take something out of the oven. r _ _ _ _ _

2 Complete the dialogue with these phrases.

SAY IT LIKE THIS!

a good idea   ~~for dinner~~   I'd like   what about   would you like

Tina: What's (1) ____for dinner____, Mum?

Mum: How about boiling some vegetables?

Tina: No, (2) _____ spaghetti.

Mum: But we had spaghetti yesterday.

Tina: That's true.

Mum: (3) _____ a pizza?

Tina: Yes, that's (4) _____. I love pizza!

Mum: (5) _____ making a salad too?

Tina: Sounds great!

3 Complete the table about yourself. Use a tick (✓) or a cross (✗).

	Like…	Don't like…
sandwiches		
chips		
spaghetti		
chocolate		
carrots		
chicken		
burgers		
eggs		

4 Tell your partner about the food that you like and don't like. Use these words to help you.

awful   delicious   disgusting   tasty

5 The phrases in bold are wrong. Write the correct phrases.

Remember!

We begin letters and emails with **Dear** ... and then **How are you?**

We use **First, Then** and **Last of all** to put our ideas in order in the letter or email. This makes it easier for the reader to follow.

We can finish with **Bye for now!** and **Love from** ... .

(1) ~~Love from Martha~~ Dear Jenny,

Hi! (2) **Bye for now!** I'm fine. I must tell you about a delicious meal I had last night.

We went to a new Indian restaurant in town. The food was really different. (3) **Then**, we had fried vegetables. They were delicious. (4) **Last of all**, we had rice with chicken and banana. It was very tasty. You must try it. (5) **First**, we had mango ice cream. You'd love it. I know you really like sweet things. Let's go to the restaurant together one day.

(6) **How are you?**

Love from Martha

6 Write an email to a friend about a disgusting meal. Use this plan to help you.

Begin like this:
Dear (your friend's name),

Answer the questions:
Where did you have the meal?
What did you eat first?
Then what did you have?
What did you have last?
What was the food like?
Must your friend have a meal there?

End like this:
Bye for now!

Love from (your name)

Review 2 — Units 3–4

1 Read the text about the Everglades National Park.

The Everglades National Park in Florida is an incredible place. President Truman opened the park on December 6th, 1947. (1) _c_

They go there because it is beautiful. Many like going kayaking through the park. (2) ____ The water is calm and the view is nice.

Kayaking isn't the only thing visitors do here. (3) ____ There are also many restaurants so they can have a meal or a snack.

(4) ____ Visitors can see them as they kayak through the park. One thing is for sure, visitors never feel bored in the Everglades.

2 Complete the text with these sentences.
- a   This is a very relaxing thing to do.
- b   The Everglades is the home of hundreds of different plants and animals.
- c   Today, one million visitors go to the park every year.
- d   They can also go sailing, cycling or for long walks and they can even play golf.

3 **Choose the correct answers.**

1 The water is very ___ in this river.
  a sure   (b) deep   c silly

2 What's ___ with Jack today?
  a wrong   b safe   c funny

3 Can you please ___ on the TV?
  a take   b turn   c try

4 Go to bed. You look really ___ .
  a fried   b tired   c interested

5 Can I have more soup? ___
  a I'm full.   b It's disgusting.
  c It's delicious.

6 I can't do this. I ___ up!
  a hill   b fry   c give

7 ___ the onion and put it in the pan.
  a Slice   b Slide   c Add

8 I don't ___ it! She's eating meat!
  a yawn   b believe   c collect

9 This film is really ___ .
  a bored   b starving
  c exciting

10 Don't cook those carrots. I eat them ___ !
  a raw   b crunchy   c safe

11 ___ the spaghetti in a litre of water.
  a Fry   b Chop   c Boil

12 Don't ___ when you're skiing. It's dangerous.
  a show off   b fall in   c hang on

4 **Choose the correct answers.**

1 Was the chef frying the eggs when the fire ___ ?
  (a) started   b was starting
  c starting

2 'Was Frank showing off again?' 'No, ___ .'
  a he was   b he wasn't
  c he didn't

3 Robbie was ___ the bridge when he fell in the river.
  a crossing   b crossed   c cross

4 Jason didn't ___ like swimming.
  a used   b use to   c use

5 Julie fell off her chair ___ she was eating.
  a when   b what   c while

6 What was Timothy doing from six o'clock ___ eight?
  a by   b until   c at

7 'Did she use to have piano lessons?' 'Yes, she ___ .'
  a used   b did   c use

8 We haven't got ___ time for a snack.
  a much   b many   c lot of

9 There are only ___ eggs in this basket.
  a a little   b not much
  c a few

10 There aren't ___ strawberries on this cake.
  a some   b no   c any

11 ___ supermarket in this town sells popcorn.
  a Every   b Some   c Any

12 There's ___ near here we can go for lunch.
  a anywhere   b everywhere
  c nowhere

5 School and Beyond

Lesson 1

1 Complete the crossword puzzle.

Across:
2 I never eat in the school ___canteen___. I prefer to make my own sandwiches.
4 The _____ rings at the end of lessons.
5 I wear a _____ when I play sport.

Down:
1 I write stories for the school _____.
3 Oh, no! We've got a _____ next week!
4 Let's go into the playground for our _____.
6 This is my first _____ at this school.

|2 C|A|N|T|E|E|N|

2 Complete the sentences with these words.

fair   classmates   strict   terms   ~~test~~   meet

1 We have a maths ___test___ next week. I'm working hard for it.
2 Our head teacher is very _____. She hasn't got favourite students.
3 I want to _____ people, but it's difficult.
4 My old head teacher was really _____. Nobody talked in her classes.
5 How many _____ are there in a school year?
6 I always sit with my _____ at lunch.

3 Match.

1 bell — e
2 cheat
3 head teacher
4 sweatshirt
5 magazine
6 canteen

a
b
c
d
e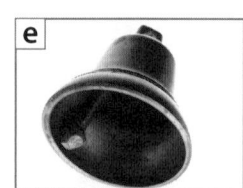
f

4 Complete the paragraph with the present perfect simple of the verbs in brackets.

The students at our school (1) __have been__ (be) very excited this week. It's nearly the end of term and we (2) _____ (study) a lot, so now we are having a party. The head teacher of our school is usually very strict, but he (3) _____ (help) us a lot. He (4) _____ (tell) us we can use the canteen for drinks and snacks. We (5) _____ (already) bought new CDs and we (6) _____ (send) invitations to all the students and teachers. Now, we are just waiting for the big day!

5 Complete the sentences with *for*, *since*, *already*, *just* or *never*. Sometimes more than one answer is possible.

1 I have been a student here __for__ five years.
2 She's tired because she has _____ had a test.
3 We have known Derek _____ last summer.
4 The term has _____ finished so we're going on holiday now.
5 Don't feed the dog again. I've _____ done it.
6 Warren always studies and he has _____ cheated on a test.

6 Look at the pictures and complete the sentences with these verbs and phrases. Use the present perfect simple.

> draw a picture   finish   ~~have lunch~~   learn   open the window   write an article

1 They __have had lunch__ in the canteen.

2 The break _____ already _____ .

3 Lisa and Victoria's mum _____ .

4 Nancy _____ for the school magazine.

5 Mrs Smith _____ of an elephant.

6 Alex _____ a lot about wild animals.

Lesson 2

1 Write the missing letters.

1 This is like a test. e <u>x</u> <u>a</u> <u>m</u>

2 You go to school for this. e _ _ _ _ _ _ _

3 This is when you don't have to do anything. t _ _ _ o _ _

4 Your teacher gives you one of these at the end of term. r _ _ _ _ _

5 Students live and study here. b _ _ _ _ _ _ _ s _ _ _ _ _

6 You get these for a test. m _ _ _ _ _

2 Write *S* (Subject), *PE* (Person) or *PL* (Place).

1 history ☐ S
2 head teacher ☐
3 geography ☐
4 nature reserve ☐
5 in the wild ☐

3 Circle the correct words.

Roxanne can't believe it! She's in the last term of her final year at school. She did not always like school. Her teachers were strict, she never got good marks and there were lots of (1) **exams** / **food**. Roxanne (2) **wanted** / **waited** to get better at geography and spent some evenings in the library. One day, she met a girl called Lisa there. Lisa was new at her school and she didn't know anyone. Lisa also had a very good (3) **understanding** / **nature** of geography and so she helped Roxanne with her work. It was the start of a very special (4) **friendship** / **report**! Roxanne and Lisa spent a lot of time together and always talked during break time. They helped each other with their homework and they never (5) **gave** / **pulled** up when lessons were difficult. They both knew it was important to do well in school, and being friends helped them to do well.

4 Complete the sentences with *ever* or *yet*.

1 I haven't been to the library ___yet___ .
2 Has she _____ passed an exam?
3 They haven't had their marks _____ .
4 Jane hasn't started school _____ .
5 Has the trainer _____ had any time off?
6 Have you _____ finished your homework before eight o'clock?

5 Look at the pictures and write questions and short answers with the present perfect simple.

1 the students / go to the forest
Have the students gone to the forest?
No, they haven't.

2 Ben and James / have a sports lesson
_____
_____

3 Mr Allison / finish the reports
_____
_____

4 Jessica / pass the exam
_____
_____

5 the students / start the exam / yet
_____
_____

6 Peter / guess the answer
_____
_____

6 Choose the correct answers.

1 We haven't _____ our emails yet.
   a write
   b wrote
   c written

2 'Have you seen my homework?' 'No, _____.'
   a I have
   b I haven't
   c haven't I

3 Have you _____ been on a school trip?
   a ever
   b yet
   c for

4 Have they _____ closed the boarding school?
   a since
   b yet
   c ever

5 The school term _____ yet.
   a has started
   b hasn't started
   c has ever started

6 'Have they left yet?' 'Yes, they _____.'
   a leave
   b haven't
   c have

Lesson 3

1 Circle the correct words.

1 I came back **school** / **home** two years ago.
2 John saw the **advert** / **town** for this job in a magazine.
3 Has your teacher **met** / **given** you lots of homework?
4 My dad has **talked** / **worked** in Spain for ten years.
5 The reporter has **interviewed** / **taught** our English teacher.

2 Look at the pictures and complete the questions with *How long* and the present perfect simple of these verbs.

~~be~~   have   know   live

1 ___How long has___ Sandra ___been___ in the library?
2 _____ they _____ a computer?
3 _____ the Wilsons _____ in this house?
4 _____ the friends _____ each other?

3 Complete the dialogue with these questions.

SAY IT LIKE THIS!

What are you bad at?
What are you good at?
What is your favourite subject?
~~Where do you go to school?~~
Who is your favourite teacher?

Dan: Hi Trevor, this is my cousin, Julie. She goes to my school.
Trevor: Hi, Julie.
Julie: Hi! Yes, Dan and I have been at the same school for four years now.
(1) ___Where do you go to school?___
Trevor: I go to school in Brighton.
Julie: (2) _____
Trevor: My favourite subject is history. What about you?
Julie: Mine is geography. I'm bad at history.
Trevor: Really! (3) _____
Julie: I'm good at maths, but I don't like it very much.
Trevor: Oh, I love maths and I'm good at it, too!
Julie: (4) _____
Trevor: I'm bad at music. I hate playing music and singing. And my music teacher, Mr Deff, is very strict.
Julie: (5) _____
Trevor: My favourite teacher is Miss Woods. She is very clever!

4 Complete the description of a school with these topic sentences.

> ~~I go to Blantyre High School in Lanarkshire.~~
> My favourite subject is German.
> There are many teachers here.
> There is one thing I don't like about my school.

Remember!

Topic sentences come at the beginning of a paragraph. They tell us what the main idea of the paragraph is.

(1) <u>I go to Blantyre High School in Lanarkshire.</u> It's a large school and it has got about 1,000 students.

(2) _____ My favourite teacher is Mr Mann. He teaches us art and he's great. He always helps his students. He's very fair and he is never strict with us.

(3) _____ I love learning new languages and German is so cool. My teacher, Mrs Schmidt, has taught for many years and her lessons are really fun.

(4) _____ The head teacher always gives us lots of exams. I hope we get a new head teacher next year!

5 Write a description of your school. Use this plan to help you.

Paragraph 1: Say what school you go to and where it is. Say how big the school is.
Paragraph 2: Say something about the teachers. Talk about your favourite teacher.
Paragraph 3: Say something about your favourite subject. Say why you like it.
Paragraph 4: Say something you don't like about your school. End the description.

6 Our Amazing Bodies

Lesson 1

1 Find the body-related words and use them to complete the sentences.

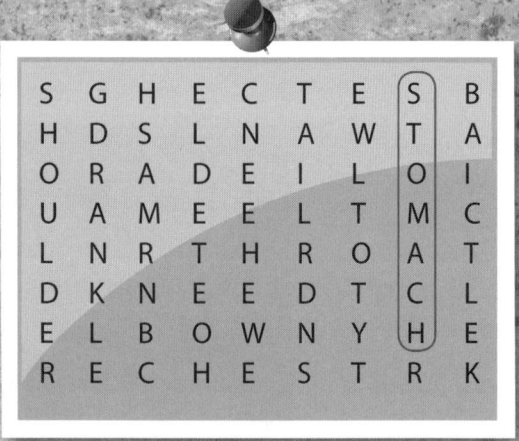

1 I ate too much and now my ___stomach___ hurts!
2 My cat has a long _____.
3 I can't speak; my _____ hurts.
4 Your _____ is at the top of your arm.
5 He coughed a lot and now his throat and _____ hurt.
6 Your _____ is in the middle of your arm.
7 My _____ and my _____ are part of my leg.

2 Match.

1 Jason rubbed his hands together.   d
2 Mrs White was in big trouble again.   ☐
3 What was that noise?   ☐
4 Be quiet!   ☐
5 There was no sign of Charles' homework.   ☐
6 Anne freed the animals.   ☐

40 UNIT 6

3 Complete the sentences with these words.

| ~~sneezes~~ | cold | thermometer | coughed | temperature | ache |

1 My mum always ___sneezes___ when she smells a flower.
2 I feel awful! I think I've caught a _____ .
3 I _____ a lot last night. I couldn't sleep.
4 You use a _____ to check your temperature.
5 I ate a lot of cake and now I have a stomach _____ .
6 What _____ is the swimming pool? Is it cold?

4 Match.

1 I broke my leg   a pulled the cat's tail.
2 When I was at school,   b so they haven't got any money.
3 Stan hasn't seen Irene   c and watched TV.
4 They haven't been at work for a month,   d I got bad reports.
5 They sat down, put their feet on the table e last week.
6 The baby has never   f since 1999.

5 Complete the sentences with the past simple or the present perfect simple of these verbs.

| break | brush | fall off | play | hurt | ~~wash~~ |

1 Karen ___has washed___ her hair twice today.
2 Guy _____ his knee. So he can't play sport.
3 The children _____ football last weekend.
4 Jack _____ his teeth last night.
5 Mrs Johnson _____ her bike three times this week.
6 Mr Russell _____ his arm yesterday.

6 Answer the questions.

1 Have you ever broken a bone? _____
2 Did you brush your hair this morning? _____
3 Did your stomach hurt last night? _____
4 Have you just got up? _____
5 Has your best friend ever stayed at your house? _____
6 Did your parents have pets when they were young? _____
7 Did you go to the dentist's last month? _____
8 Has the head teacher ever shouted at you? _____

Lesson 2

1 Match.

1. stomach ache — d
2. headache
3. cough
4. sunburn
5. bleed
6. toothache
7. temperature
8. ill

a. to feel hotter than you normally do
b. to lose blood
c. loud sound from the throat
d. pain in your stomach
e. pain in your head
f. red and hot skin
g. pain in your mouth
h. not feeling well

2 Complete the sentences with these words.

| ancient | lungs | ~~mummy~~ | injured | bleeding | tattoos | mysteries | ill |

1. Ötzi is a 5,300 year-old ___mummy___.
2. Ouch! I've _____ my leg.
3. _____ are pictures or words on the skin.
4. Ben is _____ so he can't come to school today.
5. The _____ Egyptians built pyramids for their mummies.
6. Look, my hand is _____! I cut it when I made dinner.
7. Your _____ move air in and out of your body.
8. There are lots of _____ that we don't understand in this world.

3 Circle the odd one out.

1. skin — body — (sneeze)
2. ancient — old — yesterday
3. sore — strong — injure
4. weak — ill — tattoo
5. mystery — lung — ankle

42 UNIT 6

4 Complete the sentences with possessive pronouns made from the possessive adjectives in brackets.

1 Please give this ring to Joanne. It's ___hers___ (her).
2 'Whose sweatshirt do you like?' 'I like _____ (his).'
3 That necklace isn't _____ (your).
4 'These clothes are beautiful.' 'I know, they're _____ (us)!'
5 'My head hurts!' 'So does _____ (my).'
6 He's not our leader. He's _____ (their).

5 Choose the correct answers.

1 'Can I borrow that ring?' 'No, it's not ___.'
   a my
   (b) mine
   c I

2 Look! There's ___ dentist.
   a you
   b yours
   c your

3 'My feet are freezing!' 'So ___.'
   a are mine
   b do mine
   c mine

4 Karen and Marie say the jewellery is ___.
   a they
   b their
   c theirs

5 That treasure is ___.
   a ours
   b us
   c our

6 'Your skin looks sore.' 'So ___.'
   a is hers
   b does hers
   c do she

6 Complete the sentences with *mine, yours, his, hers, ours* or *theirs*.

1 Give Jason his hat. It's ___his___ .
2 These books aren't _____ . We haven't got any books.
3 Helen, is that jewellery _____ ?
4 'Is this ring yours or Stephanie's?' 'It isn't mine, it's _____.'
5 I want my shoes back! They're _____ !
6 'Is this Mum and Dad's medicine?' 'Yes, it's _____.'

Lesson 3

1 Match.

1 school bag — e
2 stretch — ☐
3 back pain — ☐
4 doctor — ☐
5 screen — ☐
6 kid — ☐

a

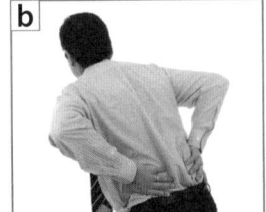
b

c

d

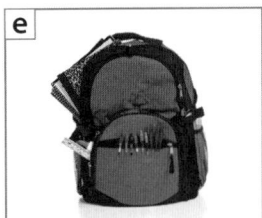
e

f

2 Look at the pictures and write the correct sentences.

SAY IT LIKE THIS!

I've got a bad cough. Is it serious? Open your mouth. Take this medicine. ~~What's the matter?~~

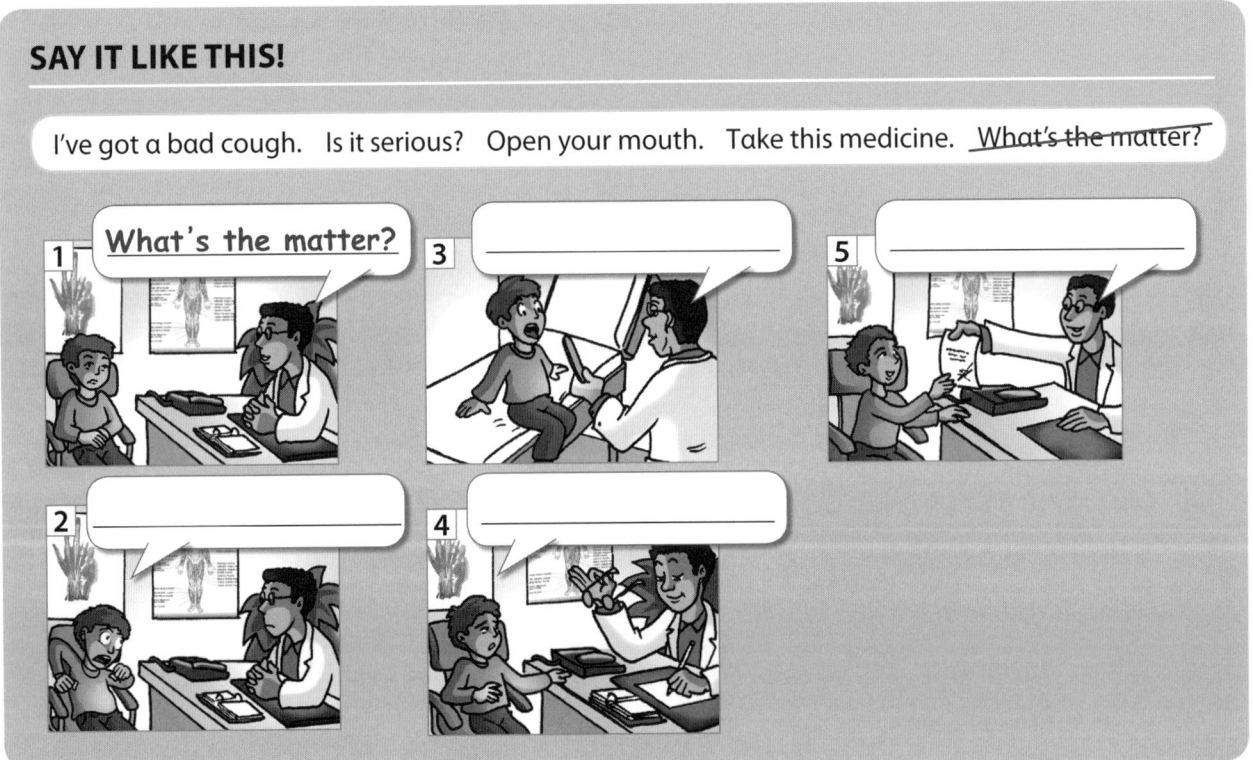

1 What's the matter?
2 ___
3 ___
4 ___
5 ___

3 Circle the words that relate to health problems.

(cough)   happy   toothache   mystery   sneeze   pain   temperature
ordinary   sore   stomach ache   throat   heavy   skin

4 Tell your partner about a health problem you have had. Use the words in Activity 3.

44   UNIT 6

5 Read the letter below and put the paragraphs in the correct order.

Hi Maggie,

[2] I've been ill for ten days now. Mum was a bit afraid, so she took me to the doctor's this morning. Do you remember Dr Foot? He's old, but he's still there! He looked at my throat and took my temperature.

[ ] Well, I'm a bit tired now. Why don't you come and see me at the weekend? You can tell me all your news then.

[ ] How are you? I'm really ill at the moment. I'm not at school, so I can write to you. I've got a nasty cold and a really sore throat.

[ ] After that, he looked into my ears. He said, 'I can't see anything'. Then he said to Mum, 'Don't worry, she's just got a cold. She doesn't need any medicine. She must rest for a few days'. So, we came back home.

See you soon!

Nelly

Remember!

There are three parts in a piece of writing: the beginning, the middle and the end. The beginning introduces the subject. The middle gives details. The end finishes the piece of writing.

6 Write a letter to a friend about your doctor or dentist. Use this plan to help you.

Begin like this:
Hi (your friend's name),

Paragraph 1
Say why you're writing. Introduce your doctor or dentist and say a few things about him / her.

Paragraphs 2 and 3
Talk about a visit to your doctor or dentist. Say what happened and what he / she was like.

Paragraph 4
Say goodbye to your friend and arrange to meet soon.

Finish like this:
See you soon!
(your name)

Review 3 — Units 5–6

1 Read the text about learning at home.

Education is very important for everyone all over the world. But must children go to school? Some people say 'no'.

In Australia, the UK and the USA, many parents teach their children at home. Sometimes this is because there isn't a school anywhere near their homes, but sometimes it is because parents believe they can give their children a better education at home.

Other people say these children won't learn much. They say they won't get the same education they can get at school. They also say these children won't make friends. In fact these children are often very clever and they are really good at exams. Their parents also make sure they play with other children.

This idea seems strange but some very famous people learnt this way. George Washington, Agatha Christie and Thomas Edison didn't go to ordinary schools. Today, actor Will Smith's children get their education at home. In fact, learning at home is very popular with a lot of people now.

2 Circle the correct words.
1 Some children don't **get an education** / **go to school**.
2 Some parents **can't pay** / **don't want** to send their children to school.
3 Children who learn at home can do well in **exams** / **homework**.
4 Some **strange** / **famous** people didn't go to school.
5 **Agatha Christie** / **Will Smith** didn't go to school.

3 **Choose the correct answers.**

1 Susan wrote this ___ for the school magazine.
   (a) article   b exam   c test

2 I hurt my arm and my ___ is sore.
   a elbow   b ankle   c knee

3 My school has three ___ each year.
   a lunch   b classes   c terms

4 Jackie always gets good ___ in tests.
   a marks   b proof   c education

5 Graham has a deep ___ of science.
   a tests   b friendship
   c understanding

6 Open your mouth, I must see your ___ .
   a shoulder   b stomach   c throat

7 We always have lunch in the school ___ .
   a library   b canteen   c lesson

8 Is the bell ___ ?
   a ringing   b learning   c sneezing

9 I'm going to the dentist because I've got ___ .
   a a temperature   b sunburn
   c toothache

10 Computer screens make my eyes ___ .
   a sore   b ill   c serious

11 The ___ Egyptians were very good at maths.
   a mystery   b ancient
   c time off

12 You should never ___ in exams.
   a steal   b cheat   c search

4 **Choose the correct answers.**

1 The school bell has just ___ .
   a ring   **(b)** rung   c rang

2 I've ___ this test before!
   a did   b do   c done

3 We've been at boarding school ___ five years now.
   a since   b already   c for

4 I've ___ taken my medicine. I don't need any more.
   a never   b just   c since

5 'Have they guessed the answer?' 'No, they ___ .'
   a haven't   b hasn't   c have

6 She hasn't given me any advice ___ .
   a yet   b never   c just

7 How long ___ a headache?
   a you have had   b have you had
   c you have

8 He ___ lunch in the canteen.
   a have eaten   b ate
   c eaten

9 ___ you spoken to the doctor yet?
   a Did   b Has   c Have

10 'Our teacher is very strict.' '___ isn't.'
   a My   b Me   c Mine

11 Please give this report to Sandy. It's ___ .
   a hers   b her   c she

12 This computer screen is ___ .
   a they   b theirs   c their

7 All Around Us

Lesson 1

1 Match.

1 Look at the volcano!
2 How long are you going to the national park for?
3 There are turtles on the beach.
4 The wildlife in Costa Rica is amazing.
5 Iguanas are a kind of big lizard.

a They live in the jungle.
b They lay eggs in the sand.
c There are lots of different animals to see.
d We're going to spend four days there.
e It's erupting. Run!

2 Complete the sentences with these words.

| branch | lay eggs | ~~leaves~~ | nest | soil | stones |

1 In autumn, the __leaves__ become yellow and brown.
2 Look! The birds have built a _____ in the tree in the garden.
3 We collected lots of _____ from the beach.
4 The _____ on that tree is very long.
5 Please clean the _____ off your boots before you come into the house.
6 Every spring, the birds _____ in their nest.

3 Write the missing letters.

1 You often find this on the beach.
2 This place is hot and there are lots of trees.
3 This thing is hard, cold and grey or brown.
4 It's very dangerous when this erupts.
5 This is a long, thin part of a tree.

s _a_ _n_ _d_
j _ _ _ _ _ _
s _ _ _ _ _
v _ _ _ _ _ _
b _ _ _ _ _

48 UNIT 7

4 Complete with these verbs. Use the future simple or *be going to*.

| buy | fall down | feed | ~~take~~ | turn on | walk |

1 Farmer Giles __is going to take__ the cows to market this week. He told me yesterday.
2 Run! That tree _____.
3 _____ she _____ the children ice cream?
4 I'm sure Philip _____ the fish at the weekend.
5 _____ you _____ the dogs tonight, Derek?
6 Clare _____ the lights in the cabin this evening.

5 Answer the questions.

1 Are you going to the beach today?
2 Will your class go on a trip this month?
3 Where will you be at five o'clock tomorrow?
4 What are you going to do after today's lesson?
5 Is your teacher going to give you a test next week?
6 Is it going to snow later?
7 What do you think will happen in the next book you read?
8 Will your class go to the zoo?

6 Look at the pictures and complete the sentences with the future simple or *be going to*.

I'm sure you __will__ take some nice photos.

I think I _____ make a sandwich.

I _____ hold the door open for you.

It _____ rain soon.

I _____ be on holiday in August.

Help me with the garden and I _____ buy you a new bike.

Lesson 2

1 Match.

1. seeds — c
2. pond — ☐
3. sip — ☐
4. creature — ☐
5. flower — ☐
6. pot — ☐

 a
 c
 e
 b
 d
 f

2 Choose the correct answers.

1. Be careful! The floor is _____ .
   a curious
   b slippery
   c massive
2. These plants need a wet and _____ climate.
   a easy
   b sticky
   c humid
3. This bottle holds a lot of _____ .
   a soils
   b meals
   c liquid
4. The plant needs more light to stay _____ .
   a light
   b alive
   c drinks
5. The leaves of this plant are _____ . Insects go there and then they can't get away.
   a sticky
   b sweet
   c brilliant

3 Complete the sentences with these words.

> stems   smell   massive   soil   trap   ~~wildlife~~

1. We must protect __wildlife__!
2. The _____ in my garden is very poor.
3. The blue whale is a _____ animal.
4. They caught the mouse with a _____ .
5. What a delicious _____!
6. Some pitcher plants have long _____ .

50 UNIT 7

4 **Complete the sentences with gerunds formed from the verbs in brackets.**

1 I can't stand ___feeding___ (feed) the cat.
2 Jason isn't very good at _____ (look after) plants.
3 We miss _____ (walk) in the fields.
4 _____ (live) in the country isn't always easy.
5 He's not interested in _____ (keep) the garden tidy.
6 My favourite thing is _____ (lie) on the grass.

5 **Look at the pictures and write T (True) or F (False).**

1 Watering the plants is a lot of fun. T
2 This plant lives by eating insects. ☐
3 Henry enjoys taking the dog for a walk. ☐
4 Tabby is good at catching mice. ☐
5 Kate doesn't miss swimming in the lake. ☐
6 Walking on slippery ice is difficult. ☐

6 **Put the words in the correct order to make sentences.**

1 doesn't / she / farm / on / working / the / like
   She doesn't like working on the farm.

2 animals / dangerous / very / feeding / is / wild
   _____

3 keeping / very / plants / good / not / at / I'm
   _____

4 telling / he / anyone / without / left
   _____

5 bad / hate / they / getting / exam marks
   _____

6 in / country / is / walking / boring / the
   _____

Lesson 3

1 Circle the correct words.

1 We gave the dog some food because it was **hungry** / **lucky**.
2 I don't like it when people are **warm** / **cruel** to animals.
3 People **bring** / **go** sick animals to the rescue centre.
4 We've got three **vets** / **pets** at home. Two rabbits and a cat.
5 My dog was in a(n) **rescue** / **accident** yesterday. He's got a broken leg.

2 Choose the correct answers.

1 You've got a cute hamster, _____?
  a haven't you
  b don't you
  c isn't it
2 She's taking the dog to the Rescue Centre, _____?
  a hasn't she
  b doesn't she
  c isn't she
3 My pet is very cuddly, _____?
  a is it
  b isn't it
  c hasn't it
4 They didn't clean the rabbit's hutch, _____?
  a were they
  b could they
  c did they
5 The vet isn't going to give the cat any medicine, _____?
  a will she
  b is it
  c is she
6 The rabbit _____ really cute, wasn't it?
  a is
  b was
  c did
7 Ron's pets are very furry, aren't _____?
  a they
  b he
  c it
8 They must feed the animals three times a day, _____?
  a can they
  b must they
  c mustn't they

3 Complete the dialogue with these words.

SAY IT LIKE THIS!

fish   cuddly   fast   furry   hutch   rabbit

Toby: I got a new pet from the Pet Rescue Centre yesterday.
Greta: Wow! Tell me more about it.
Toby: OK, guess what animal it is. My pet is very (1) __cuddly__. It wants me to hold it all day.
Greta: Uh huh.
Toby: It runs very (2) _____ and it can jump.
Greta: Does it eat (3) _____?
Toby: No, it doesn't.
Greta: OK, so it isn't a cat!
Toby: No, it isn't a cat. But it's very (4) _____ like a cat.
Greta: Has your pet got big ears?
Toby: Yes, it has!
Greta: Your pet lives in a (5) _____, doesn't it?
Toby: Yes!
Greta: Your pet is a (6) _____!
Toby: That's right!

4 Read the description of a pet below. Find the punctuation and capital letter mistakes and correct them.

> My best friend is my cat. She's called Nelly and she's six years old. Nelly is very furry and cuddly.
>
> We do everything together. we play in the garden and we listen to music together in my bedroom. She makes me laugh when I'm sad. She's fantastic?
>
> I feed Nelly in our garden. She likes biscuits fish, vegetables and cat food. but her favourite food is Fish. All cats love eating fish, don't they!
>
> I love looking after Nelly. When she is tired, I put her in her basket. It's in my living room. It's great having a cat isn't it?

Remember!

Punctuation and capital letters

We use capital letters to begin:
- names. **J**oanne
- places. **L**os **A**ngeles
- sentences. **S**he's taking the mouse to the vet's.

Sentences end with a full stop or an exclamation mark for emphasis.

The garden looks lovely.
Don't play in the garden!

Questions end with a question mark.
Are you leaving tomorrow?

We use commas to separate:
- words in a list: cats, dogs, lizards and mice
- question tags from the rest of a sentence:

    The hamster's sick, isn't it?

5 Write a description of your pet or a friend's pet. Use this plan to help you.

Paragraph 1
Say what kind of pet you or your friend have got. Describe what it looks like.

Paragraph 2
Say what you do or your friend does with the pet.

Paragraph 3
Say what the pet likes.

Paragraph 4
Say how you feel or how your friend feels about the pet and end the description.

8 Protecting the Planet

Lesson 1

1 Find the environment-related words and use them to complete the sentences.

```
G O A K S S Y S T E M
S S E Y B A P M N D P
S M P A W T K M P B O
A E L D U M P R B I N
B L A D F B W E U L P
M L S R M A S S O P S
P B T D R T O I W D L
C A I S A T S M D J L
X D C D O E P B A T R
A G B O L R E A K P M
V (C A N) O Y R P L S M
E A G P O S I D M P I
```

1 I don't want a bottle of lemonade, I want a ___can___ .

2 Don't use a _____ for your shopping. Use a box.

3 They _____ all the rubbish in this landfill.

4 Your mobile phone isn't working because there's no _____ in it.

5 There's a _____ to collect rainwater in this park.

6 Landfills usually _____.

2 Circle the correct words.

1 Let's get out of here, it **improves** /(**smells**) bad.

2 All our rubbish goes to the **landfill** / **tree**.

3 I put all my books in a **cardboard** / **electronics** box.

4 The table was **covered** / **smelled** with plates of food.

5 Let's work hard to **find** / **improve** the environment.

3 Complete the sentences with these words.

| covered   environmental   newspaper   ~~batteries~~   cans   electronics |

1 This torch has got new ___batteries___ in it.

2 I read an interesting article in the _____ yesterday.

3 The _____ centre teaches people about recycling.

4 I'm interested in _____, like smartphones and computers.

5 Oh no! The dog is _____ in mud.

6 It's important to reuse _____ and plastic bags.

4 Look at the pictures and complete the first conditional sentences with these phrases.

> not hurt the environment   not find us   not use plastic bags
> see lots of wild animals   swim in the pool   ~~throw away the rubbish~~

1 If they _throw away the rubbish_ , the kitchen won't smell bad.

2 If she _____ _____, she will help the environment.

3 If we hide in that house, they _____ _____.

4 If I go to the jungle, I'll _____ _____.

5 If he puts the newspapers in the correct bin, he _____ _____.

6 If they _____, they won't have to leave the hotel.

5 Circle the correct words.

1 If we **won't** / **don't** recycle rubbish, the environment will be in danger.
2 Visitors **are coming** / **will come** to our beaches if we start keeping them clean.
3 If you take the cans to the recycling bin, I **give** / **will give** you a present.
4 How **will they** / **do they** read the newspaper if we put it in the recycling bin?
5 I **don't give** / **won't give** you our old clothes if you don't want them.

6 Complete the first conditional sentences with the verbs in brackets.

Interviewer: Today, I'm speaking to Rita West. She's the leader of Save the Environment Now! Rita, why do we need to 'save the environment now'?

Rita: Well, John, if we (1) _don't look after_ (not look after) the environment now, we (2) _____ (lose) many places.

Interviewer: What (3) _____ (happen) if we (4) _____ (lose) these places?

Rita: Good question. Firstly, some animals (5) _____ (not have) any homes if we (6) _____ (not protect) these areas. If these animals (7) _____ (die), people (8) _____ (be) in great danger, too.

Interviewer: (9) _____ it _____ (make) any difference if we (10) _____ (recycle) things?

Rita: Of course, it will make a huge difference. But reusing things is not the only thing we must do. We must change the way we live and the way we think!

Lesson 2

1 Match.

1. tap water — f
2. oil
3. petrol
4. destroy
5. recycle
6. pollute

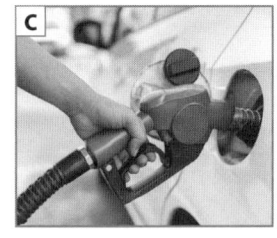

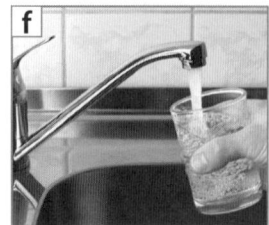

2 Complete the webpage with these words.

oil   pollute   products   ~~recycle~~   throw away

Go green, make a difference!
Do you want to help the environment, but don't know how? Here is some useful advice!
- (1) __Recycle__ bottles, paper and cans.
- Buy only green (2) _____ .
- Don't (3) _____ things you can recycle.
- Don't (4) _____ the land, sea or air.
- Don't waste (5) _____ . Don't buy lots of plastic products.

3 Circle the correct words.

1. Bottled water costs money, but tap water is almost **free** / **waste**.
2. People often use air **conditioning** / **products** to cool their homes in the summer.
3. Be **free** / **green** and help the environment!
4. A lot of food is **polluted** / **wasted** every day.
5. You can keep cool on a hot day with a **fan** / **oil**.

4 Complete the second conditional sentences with the verbs in brackets.

1. If there __weren't__ (not be) any recycling bins in my neighbourhood, I __would start__ (start) a recycling group.
2. _____ you _____ (build) a house if I _____ (give) you 14,000 plastic bottles?
3. You _____ (help) the environment if you _____ (use) that plastic bag again.
4. What _____ (happen) to the rainforest if farmers _____ (need) more land for cows?
5. If everyone _____ (sit) in the dark for one hour, we _____ (save) a lot of energy.
6. The environment _____ (not be) in danger if more people _____ (go) green.

5 Choose the correct answers.

1. If everyone _____ the beaches, they would be nice.
   a looks after
   b will look after
   c looked after

2. If I _____ you, I'd buy green products.
   a weren't
   b were
   c would be

3. _____ a difference if I wrote an article about pollution?
   a Would it make
   b Does it make
   c Did it make

4. If he _____ a shower four times a day, he would save water.
   a wouldn't have
   b didn't have
   c hadn't

5. If they polluted the river, all the wildlife _____ .
   a is dead
   b died
   c would die

6. Would Karen go there if they _____ green products?
   a don't sell
   b didn't sell
   c wouldn't sell

6 Answer the questions with the second conditional. Use the words in brackets.

1. What would your mum do if you told her to recycle more? (listen to me)
   If I told my mum to recycle more, she would listen to me.

2. What would you do if you saw people polluting the beach? (shout at them)
   _____

3. What would you do if you were the leader of an environmental group? (write an article)
   _____

4. What would happen if we reused things? (not have lots of rubbish)
   _____

5. What would they do if they owned a supermarket? (sell only green products)
   _____

6. How would you feel if you lived next to a rubbish dump? (not be happy)
   _____

Lesson 3

1 Match.

1. Kim's breathing in oxygen. — b
2. Kim's wasting energy. — ☐
3. Kim's planting a tree. — ☐
4. Kim's tap is dripping. — ☐
5. Kim's throwing away food. — ☐
6. The shade is keeping Kim cool. — ☐

2 Look at the pictures and complete the sentences with these phrases.

SAY IT LIKE THIS!

~~never pollute the forest~~   never waste food   recycle plastic bottles   ride our bikes   throw away rubbish

1. We **never pollute the forest**.
2. We _____.
3. We _____.
4. I _____.
5. We _____.

3 Tell your partner about what you do for the environment.

4 Read the email and circle the correct words.

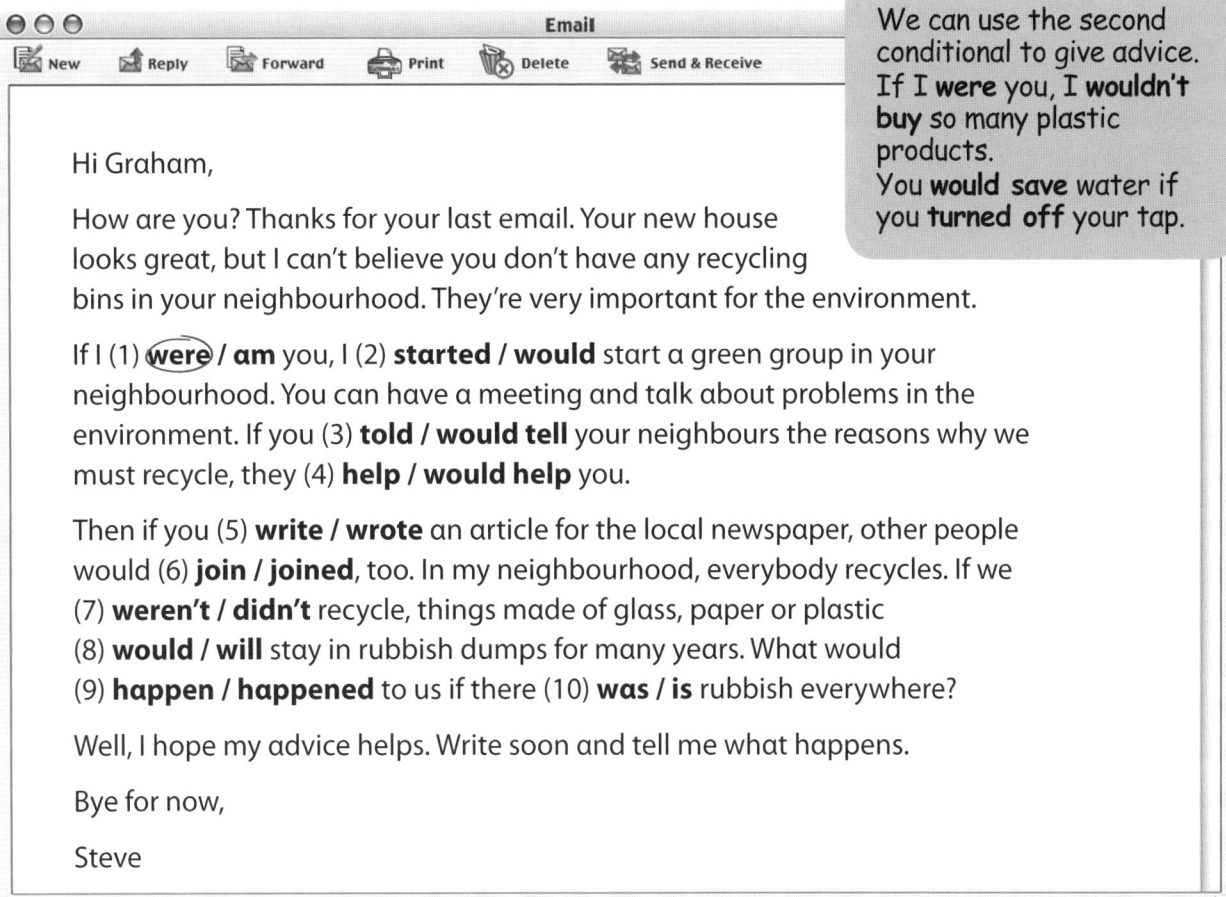

Remember!
We can use the second conditional to give advice.
If I **were** you, I **wouldn't buy** so many plastic products.
You **would save** water if you **turned off** your tap.

Hi Graham,

How are you? Thanks for your last email. Your new house looks great, but I can't believe you don't have any recycling bins in your neighbourhood. They're very important for the environment.

If I (1) **were** / **am** you, I (2) **started** / **would** start a green group in your neighbourhood. You can have a meeting and talk about problems in the environment. If you (3) **told** / **would tell** your neighbours the reasons why we must recycle, they (4) **help** / **would help** you.

Then if you (5) **write** / **wrote** an article for the local newspaper, other people would (6) **join** / **joined**, too. In my neighbourhood, everybody recycles. If we (7) **weren't** / **didn't** recycle, things made of glass, paper or plastic (8) **would** / **will** stay in rubbish dumps for many years. What would (9) **happen** / **happened** to us if there (10) **was** / **is** rubbish everywhere?

Well, I hope my advice helps. Write soon and tell me what happens.

Bye for now,

Steve

5 Write an email to a friend giving advice about how to help the environment. Use this plan to help you.

Begin like this:
Hi (your friend's name),

Paragraph 1
Ask how your friend is and talk about his / her last email. Say something about a problem with the environment that your friend has.

Paragraphs 2 and 3
Give your friend advice to help with the problem.

Paragraph 4
End the email and ask your friend to write back.

Finish like this:
Bye for now,
(your name)

Review 4 — Units 7–8

1 Read the text about the environment.

We all know that nature and the environment are in danger. We are polluting our world and this means that the climate is changing and Earth is becoming warmer. So what are people doing about it?

Scientists never stop studying the land, the air and the sea. They want to find out what is happening and how we are destroying them. In 2005, scientists from America and Sweden studied the icy sea in Canada Basin. This is the sea between Alaska and the North Pole. The scientists used two massive boats, the *Healy* and the *Oden*. These boats can break ice as they move.

When they reached the places they wanted to study, divers jumped into the water. They collected water in glass bottles and they studied it. The scientists wanted to know if the sea in Canada Basin was becoming warmer. Jim Swift was one of the scientists on the *Healy*. He says that there was a lot more ice in Canada Basin 40 years ago, and the tests they did are proof of this.

So, let's stop wasting energy and start protecting the environment!

2 Answer the questions.

1 What is happening to Earth because of pollution? It is becoming warmer.

2 What do scientists always study? _____

3 What is Canada Basin? _____

4 What is special about the *Healy* and the *Oden*? _____

5 What did divers collect from Canada Basin? _____

6 Who is Jim Swift? _____

3 **Choose the correct answers.**

1 We've got a ___ in the garden with rabbits in it.
   a trap   (b) hutch   c pond
2 He's a very ___ person.
   a curious   b sticky   c stone
3 We should never ___ the environment.
   a pollute   b stink   c waste
4 Humans ___ air.
   a turn on   b breathe in   c save
5 There's a cat on the ___ of our tree.
   a nest   b leaf   c branch
6 The ___ makes the room cool.
   a battery   b fan   c plastic bag

7 Look at the poor little ___ in its basket.
   a wildlife   b criminal   c creature
8 Walking on ice can be very ___ .
   a sticky   b furry   c slippery
9 This ___ will help us catch the mouse.
   a trap   b seed   c light
10 Elephants are ___ , grey animals.
   a erupt   b massive   c humid
11 Don't ___ that glass bottle. You can recycle it.
   a throw away   b discover   c hide
12 Please put your rubbish in the ___ at the end of the street.
   a litter bin   b money box   c plastic bag

4 **Choose the correct answers.**

1 They're ___ destroy that rubbish tomorrow.
   (a) going to   b will   c going
2 ___ Charles take the cat to the rescue centre?
   a Is   b Will   c Is he going
3 I'm sure the climate ___ in the next hundred years.
   a is changing   b changes   c will change
4 I hate ___ food.
   a to waste   b wasting   c waste
5 ___ plants is something I enjoy.
   a To water   b Water   c Watering
6 Dina thinks about the environment, ___ she?
   a hasn't   b doesn't   c won't

7 I didn't hurt your cat, ___?
   a did I   b was I   c didn't I
8 They've recycled those boxes, ___ they?
   a didn't   b haven't   c aren't
9 Will you tidy your room if I ___ you a new bike?
   a buy   b will buy   c am buying
10 If I were you, I ___ that creature!
   a wouldn't hurt   b won't hurt   c didn't hurt
11 If you recycle, you ___ the environment.
   a are helping   b are going to help   c will help
12 Would she call the police if they ___ the wild animals?
   a did steal   b stole   c would steal

61

9 City Life

Lesson 1

1 Match.

1. turn right / left — **e**
2. go around the corner — ☐
3. cross the road — ☐
4. go past — ☐
5. go straight on — ☐

a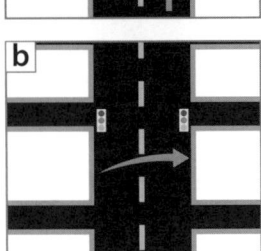
b
c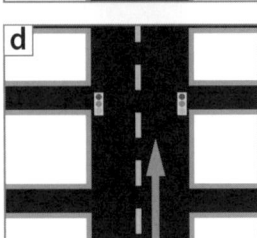
d
e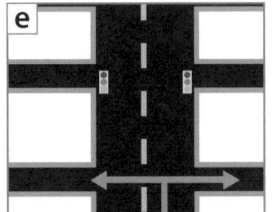

2 Circle the correct words.

1. My sister **designs** / **follows** gardens for her job.
2. If you follow the **location** / **directions**, you'll be there in ten minutes.
3. There is a lot of **sight** / **information** at the environmental centre.
4. Don't worry if you lose your way. Your phone will know your **location** / **design**.
5. Turn right and then **go** / **follow** the road to the library.
6. London has a lot of famous **sights** / **information**.

3 Complete the sentences with these words.

| on | cross | go | right | round | ~~turn~~ |

1. _____Turn_____ left at the supermarket.
2. _____ the road at the traffic lights.
3. Turn _____ at the library.
4. When you cross Merry Lane, go straight _____ .
5. If you go _____ the corner, you will see the bank.
6. _____ past the park to the school.

62 UNIT 9

4 Complete the sentences with the correct form of *have to* and these verbs.

> be   ~~cross~~   get away   go   not ask   not do

1 '___Do___ we ___have to cross___ the road at the traffic lights?' 'Yes, we do.'
2 '_____ you _____ to the supermarket yesterday?' 'No, I didn't.'
3 This cave is awful! We _____ from here.
4 Sarah found the school easily. She _____ the way.
5 I _____ my homework tonight. It's the weekend!
6 We _____ careful because this is a busy road.

5 Complete the sentences with *must, mustn't, don't have to* or *doesn't have to*.

1 She ___must___ get to the café quickly because Ron's waiting for her there.
2 You _____ go to the post office because I went this morning.
3 You _____ drive now. The traffic light is red.
4 We don't want to miss the bus, so we _____ hurry.
5 He _____ take a taxi because I can drive him there.
6 You _____ go to the park today. Everything is wet from the rain.

6 Choose the correct answers.

1 Do we _____ go to the bank later?
   a must
   (b) have to
   c have

2 _____ I buy a bus ticket tomorrow?
   a Have
   b Must
   c Did

3 'Must we come with you to the supermarket?' 'Yes, you _____ .'
   a must
   b do
   c mustn't

4 Jerry _____ to turn left at the café in Baker Street.
   a has
   b must
   c hasn't

5 They _____ go to the supermarket. I can go later.
   a mustn't
   b have to
   c don't have to

6 You _____ walk through the park at night. It's dangerous.
   a don't have to
   b mustn't
   c must

63

Lesson 2

1 Complete the crossword puzzle.

Across
1. You go up and down these outside.
2. People keep their money in this place.
4. This is a large open space in the centre of a city.
5. This is a boat that you can take to another place.
6. You can buy clothes, shoes, books, toys and food in this place.

1 S T E P S

Down
1. This is a very tall building.
3. You buy this to get into the theatre or cinema.

2 Choose the correct answers.

1. This cake is very _____ but it's delicious.
   - (a) expensive
   - b plastic
   - c curious

2. There are so many _____ you can see in this city.
   - a sights
   - b rides
   - c ferries

3. There's a great art _____ at the Metropolitan Museum.
   - a park
   - b district
   - c collection

4. Did you _____ in the lake last week?
   - a spend
   - b fish
   - c try

5. Is London a _____ place to live?
   - a cheap
   - b square
   - c tall

6. Do you want to _____ snowboarding this weekend?
   - a fish
   - b run
   - c try

3 Complete the sentences with these words.

| fish | ticket | spend | ~~expensive~~ | try | see |

1. Is the jacket cheap or is it _expensive_ ?
2. We always _____ in the lake in summer.
3. Let's buy a _____ for the ferry.
4. Here, _____ this pizza. It's delicious!
5. How much money did you _____?
6. Can I _____ your music collection?

64 UNIT 9

4 Complete the paragraph with *can, can't, could* or *couldn't*.

Jack's very happy because his family (1) ___can___ go on holiday this year. Last year, they (2) _____ go anywhere because they were very busy. This year, they (3) _____ go somewhere expensive because they haven't got a lot of money. Jack wants to go to Egypt because you (4) _____ see a lot of interesting things there, but his mum (5) _____ go by plane because she's scared of flying. They will have to go somewhere by train or car. The last time they went on holiday, they went to Italy by car. They stayed in Rome for ten days and they (6) _____ see the Colosseum from their hotel. They had a wonderful time, so maybe they will go back again this year.

5 Read the sentences and write *T* (True) or *F* (False).

1 Today, crossing the road is easy. ☐ T
2 In the past, you could recycle rubbish in the square. ☐
3 Today, you can't listen to music in the square. ☐
4 In the past, you couldn't see a lot of rubbish in the square. ☐
5 In the past, you could go on a tour of the square. ☐

Past

Present

6 Answer the questions.

1 Could you write when you were five years old? _____
2 Can students have lessons in the park? _____
3 Can cats go to the cinema? _____
4 Could people drive cars 300 years ago? _____
5 Could you walk to the park when you were ten months old? _____
6 Could you go into town with your friends when you were seven? _____

Lesson 3

1 Complete the sentences with these words.

> ~~comfortable~~   free   guide
> jogging   sure   swimming costume

1. My feet hurt because my shoes aren't very ___comfortable___ .
2. Don't forget your _____ . We might go to the beach.
3. Make _____ you visit Petra when you go to Jordan.
4. Please buy a city _____ for Paris before we leave.
5. Brian always goes _____ in Central Park at the weekend.
6. You don't have to pay for the ferry to the island. It's _____ .

2 Circle the correct words.

1. Simon **should** / **(might)** go to Egypt, but he's not sure yet.
2. You **might not** / **shouldn't** like the food in Glasgow.
3. She **shouldn't** / **might not** go on a tour of the city without a guide. It's dangerous.
4. **Should** / **Might** we visit the Louvre or the Pompidou Centre?
5. This bridge **might** / **should** fall so don't cross it.
6. You **should** / **might** be careful when you walk along the river.
7. We **shouldn't** / **might not** have a picnic today. We haven't decided yet.
8. Visitors **might** / **should** eat at the Chinese restaurant because the food's fantastic.

3 Complete the dialogue with these words. Use the map to help you.

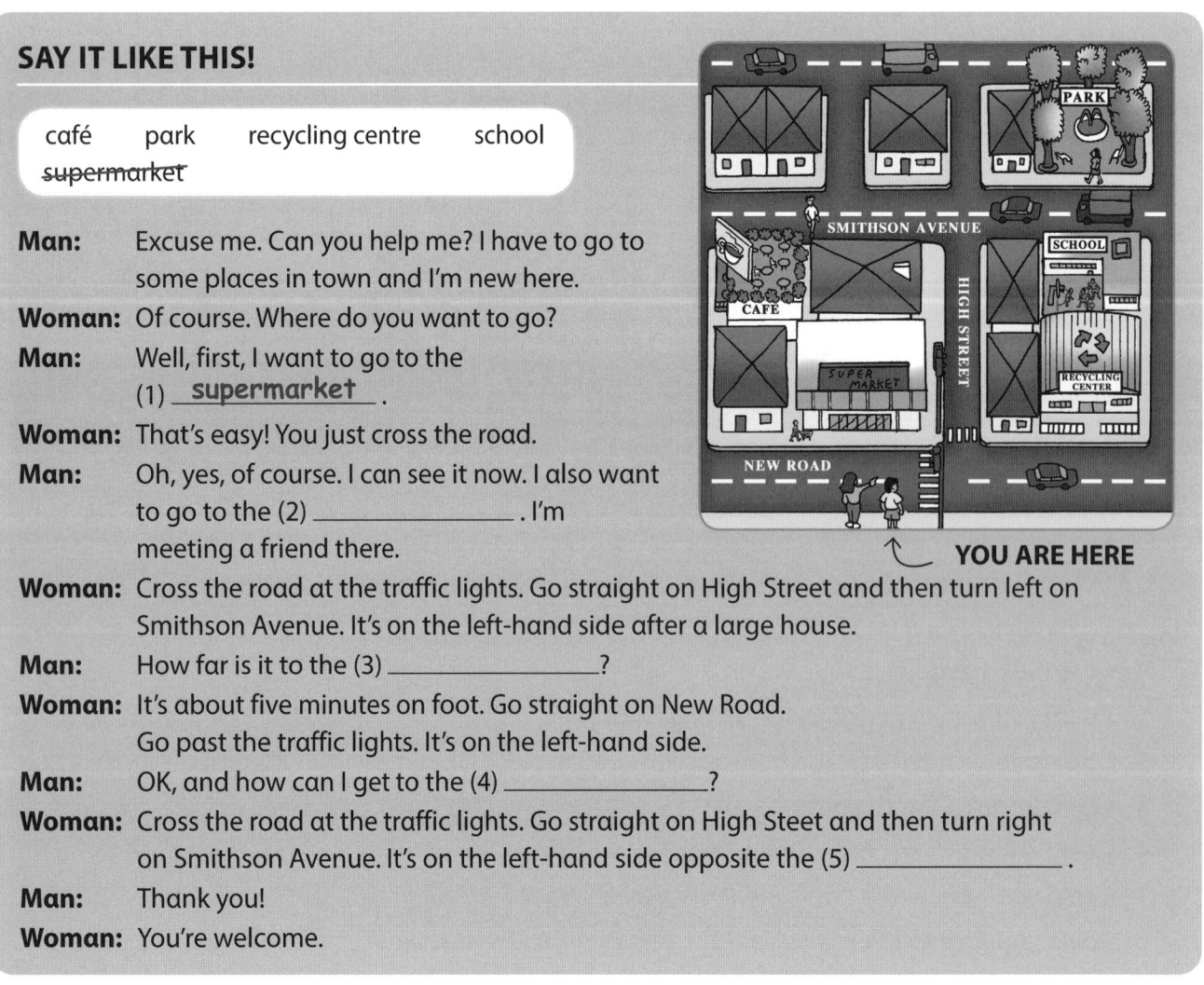

SAY IT LIKE THIS!

> café   park   recycling centre   school
> ~~supermarket~~

Man: Excuse me. Can you help me? I have to go to some places in town and I'm new here.
Woman: Of course. Where do you want to go?
Man: Well, first, I want to go to the (1) ___supermarket___ .
Woman: That's easy! You just cross the road.
Man: Oh, yes, of course. I can see it now. I also want to go to the (2) _____ . I'm meeting a friend there.
Woman: Cross the road at the traffic lights. Go straight on High Street and then turn left on Smithson Avenue. It's on the left-hand side after a large house.
Man: How far is it to the (3) _____ ?
Woman: It's about five minutes on foot. Go straight on New Road. Go past the traffic lights. It's on the left-hand side.
Man: OK, and how can I get to the (4) _____ ?
Woman: Cross the road at the traffic lights. Go straight on High Steet and then turn right on Smithson Avenue. It's on the left-hand side opposite the (5) _____ .
Man: Thank you!
Woman: You're welcome.

4 Read Mike's postcard and correct the mistakes in the order of adjectives.

Hi Chris,

How are you? I'm on holiday in a ~~Greek lovely town~~ lovely, Greek town called Nafplio.

Nafplio is an interesting little town with lots of beautiful sights. There's an old amazing castle at the top of a huge rock. It's called the Palamidi and you can see it from all around the town. There's another castle in the middle of the sea. It's called the Bourtzi and you have to go there by boat. It's a beautiful stone building.

There's also a huge fantastic square. You can have a big nice ice cream or try the local delicious food in the restaurants there. I had some chewy white tasty fish last night in one of the restaurants. I loved it!

You should visit Nafplio. You'll have a great time here.

See you soon!

Mike

Remember!

When there are many adjectives before a noun, we put them in this order:

opinion	brilliant
size	massive
age	ancient
shape	square
colour	orange
origin	Welsh
material	glass

5 Write a postcard to a friend describing a town. Use this plan to help you.

Begin like this:
Hi (your friend's name),

Paragraph 1
Ask your friend how he / she is. Say which town you are visiting.

Paragraph 2
Describe the town and some of the sights there.

Paragraph 3
Say what you can do / eat in the town.

Paragraph 4
Tell your friend to visit the town too.

Finish like this:
See you soon!
(your name)

10 Share and Enjoy

Lesson 1

1 Find the computer-related words and use them to complete the sentences.

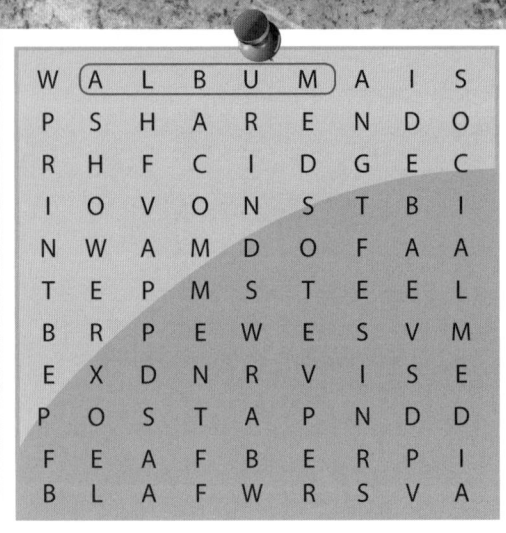

1 My favourite photos are all in this ___album___.
2 Why did you _____ your homework on yellow paper?
3 Can you _____ your holiday photos with us? We want to see them!
4 I wrote a _____ about your new photos today.
5 I _____ a new story on the Internet every day.
6 I love _____ ! It's fun to see photos and talk to your friends online.
7 Did I _____ you my new computer?
8 This new _____ on my phone helps me to eat healthy food.

2 Circle the correct words.

1 There are three new **comments** / **uploads** about my photos.
2 My friends often **print** / **post** photos to social media.
3 We look at our **digital** / **app** photos on our phones.
4 The **album** / **Internet** has a lot of information on it.
5 I take photos of my lunch and then I **upload** / **comment** them to social media.
6 He likes writing funny **comments** / **digital** on websites.
7 Which film do you want to watch? I'll **download** / **post** it now.
8 I don't like digital photos. I prefer to **comment** / **print** them.

3 Write the missing letters.

1 You do this when you want something on paper. p r i n t
2 This is something you download onto your smartphone. a _ _
3 You write this about someone's post on social media. c _ _ _ _ _ _
4 You keep lots of photos in this. a _ _ _ _
5 You can find lots of information on this. I _ _ _ _ _ _ _

4 Circle the correct words.

1 The songs **is listened to** / **listens to** by thousands of people every day.
2 She **gives** / **is given** a free music magazine every month.
3 Piano music isn't **play** / **played** on this station.
4 Is the news **shown** / **show** on this channel?
5 The musicians aren't **pay** / **paid** every week.

5 Complete with the past and present simple passive of the verbs in brackets.

1 The photos __are uploaded__ (upload) every weekend.
2 _____ this film _____ (show) every year?
3 I _____ (see) by millions of people every day on my new programme.
4 These smartphones _____ (not make) by a Japanese company.
5 This comment _____ (post) by my brother.
6 _____ you _____ (pay) at the end of every show?
7 The story _____ (not print) in the newspaper today.
8 These games _____ (played) by children everywhere.

6 Put the words in the correct order.

1 ? / money / much / spent / on / is / games
__Is much money spent on games?__

2 are / on / shared / stories / social media
_____

3 songs / chosen / us / the / aren't / by
_____

4 are / by / fans / sent / letters / the
_____

5 ? / doors / are / locked / the / every night
_____

6 app / by / isn't / many / used / people / this
_____

Lesson 2

1 Circle the correct words.

1 There's a new **screen** / **(reality)** show on this channel.
2 A man called Charles Babbage **invented** / **informed** the first computer in the 1830s.
3 Carl's just written a very funny **sitcom** / **news**.
4 I **watch** / **imagine** this new reality show will be very popular.
5 This documentary informs and **shows** / **entertains** us.

2 Complete the sentences with these words.

> quality   documentaries   ~~news~~   technology   programme

1 My parents watch the ____news____ every night.
2 _____ has really changed since my grandma was young.
3 My favourite TV _____ is a cartoon about science.
4 The Discovery Channel shows a lot of _____ .
5 DVDs are better _____ than tapes.

3 Write the missing letters.

1 Children enjoy watching this.   c _a_ _r_ _t_ _o_ _o_ _n_
2 There are lots of programmes in a…   s _ _ _ _ _
3 Actors and musicians do this.   e _ _ _ _ _ _ _ _
4 This is a programme about real people.   r _ _ _ _ _ _ _ _ _ _
5 This is how good or bad something is.   q _ _ _ _ _ _
6 People do this on video cameras.   r _ _ _ _ _

4 Match.

1 The news — c wasn't read by Trevor tonight.
2 The photographer — e was bought at Harvey's.
3 These photos — a were taken in a studio.
4 Mobile phones — b were invented in 1973.
5 The actors — d weren't informed about the problem.
6 This massive TV — f was given a difficult job.

(Note: matches based on line drawn: 1–c, 2–e shown by connecting line; remaining inferred: 3–a, 4–b, 5–d, 6–f)

5 Complete the paragraph with the past simple passive of the verbs in brackets.

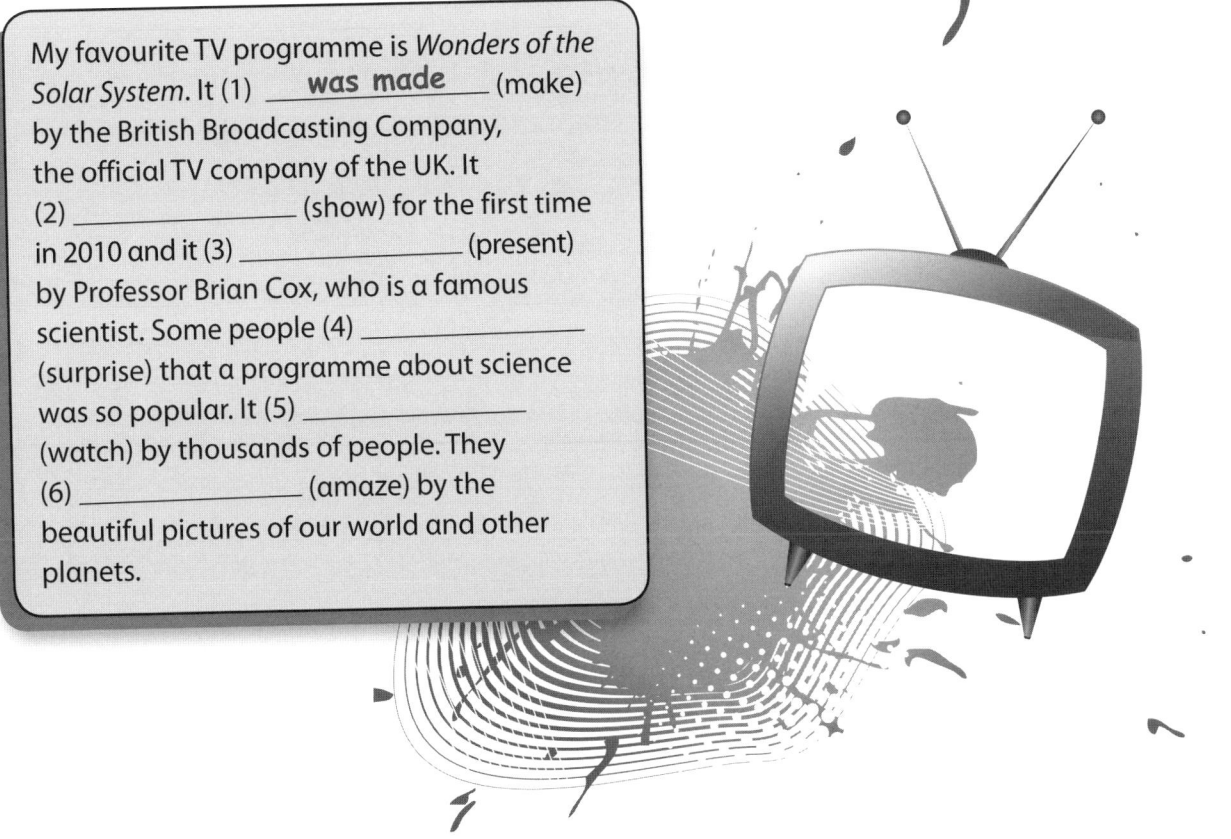

My favourite TV programme is *Wonders of the Solar System*. It (1) __was made__ (make) by the British Broadcasting Company, the official TV company of the UK. It (2) _____ (show) for the first time in 2010 and it (3) _____ (present) by Professor Brian Cox, who is a famous scientist. Some people (4) _____ (surprise) that a programme about science was so popular. It (5) _____ (watch) by thousands of people. They (6) _____ (amaze) by the beautiful pictures of our world and other planets.

6 Complete with the past simple passive of these verbs.

| give | ~~invent~~ | interview | not show | write | wash |

1 When __were__ DVDs first __invented__ ?
2 That sitcom _____ by my best friend!
3 We _____ a new TV as a present.
4 My neighbour _____ for the photographer's job.
5 The cartoon _____ before nine o'clock.
6 _____ the clothes _____ after the show?

Lesson 3

1 Complete the sentences with these words.

> voice   practise   ~~channel~~   reviews   advertise

1 My sister's got her own video ___channel___.
   She's got lots of followers.
2 I write _____ of music and films and post them online.
3 I want to _____ my new sitcom so that lots of people watch it.
4 Have you listened to Alicia's new song? She's got a great _____.
5 You need to _____ the guitar before you can post your song.

2 Complete the table about you.

	You	Your partner
How often do you listen to the radio?		
Who is your favourite DJ?		
What programmes do you listen to?		
What programmes can't you stand?		
When do you listen to the radio?		
How many radios are there in your house?		

3 Now interview your partner about the radio and complete the table.

4 Match.

SAY IT LIKE THIS!

1 My favourite show is   a film?
2 Do you prefer watching TV   b to comedy films.
3 I can't stand   c a reality show.
4 I prefer cartoons   d to watching films?
5 What is your favourite   e documentaries.
6 I prefer reading books   f to listening to the radio.

5 Read this film review and find and correct the spelling mistakes.

My favourite film is called *Good Morning Vietnam*. It is a comedy about an American DJ in Vietnam in the 1960s. At that time, people were fighting each other in that country.

In the film, acter Robin Williams plays the role of DJ Adrian Cronauer. Cronauer's shows are very funny and he plays great rock sogns. He begins evry show by shouting 'Good morning Vietnam'. Everyone loves his show. His boss, Dickerson, can't stand the way he talks or the msic he plays. He thinks Cronauer should be more sirious. In the end, Cronauer is sent away from Saigon. Before he leaves, he asks his friend Garlick to continue his programme. Garlick's first show begins with Cronauer shouting 'Goodbye Vietnam'.

I really enjoyed *Good Morning Vietnam* becuase the acting is fantastic and I love the music. It's a very entertaining and funny film, but there are some scarry bits in it. If you like music, you'll love it.

Remember!

Always read your writing and check your spelling carefully.

6 Write a review about your favourite film. Use this plan to help you.

Paragraph 1
Say what the name of the film is and what kind of film it is.

Paragraph 2
Say who the main character is and what happens in the film.

Paragraph 3
Say why you like the film.

Review 5 Units 9–10

1 **Read the text about advertising.**

Advertising has changed a lot since the first advert was shown on American TV in 1941. Today we can see adverts all around us. They're found on buses, trains and on the top of buildings.

If you go to Shanghai, in China, you will see something amazing. Boats are used for advertising! In the area of Pudong, boats sail up and down the river with massive screens on them. It's like being at the cinema, but you're outside and the screens are moving! These screens show all kinds of adverts.

A 1,500 foot screen was first seen in Shanghai in the year 2006. It may seem strange to tourists, but not to local people. Screens show adverts in lots of unusual places all over the city. This isn't surprising because China has got over 72,000 advertising companies.

It all started with advertising on television, but new technology is changing our towns and cities all the time. You can see adverts on screens in big cities all around the world.

2 **Answer the questions.**

1 What was shown on American TV for the first time in 1941?
   <u>an advert</u>

2 Where can you see adverts in Shanghai but not in other cities?
   _____

3 What is 1,500 feet?
   _____

4 What are all over the city?
   _____

5 How many advertising companies are there in China?
   _____

3 **Choose the correct answers.**

1 Let's go ___ on.
   a follow   b invent
   ĉ straight

2 ___ the road at the traffic lights.
   a Cross   b Turn
   c Go straight

3 My favourite TV show is a ___ .
   a sitcom   b ferry
   c album

4 How much is the ___ for the cinema?
   a skyscraper   b ticket
   c collection

5 I posted a ___ on your website today.
   a share   b face
   c comment

6 I saw an interesting ___ about living in big cities.
   a song   b documentary
   c advert

7 I like this shop. It's fun and ___ .
   a invented   b cheap
   c uploaded

8 Let's go to the ___ . I need a new hat.
   a museum   b skyscraper
   c shopping centre

9 Do you have to go up ___ to the museum?
   a corners   b steps
   c traffic lights

10 Let's ___ that new song you like.
   a download   b write
   c lose

11 There's a(n) ___ of unusual insects.
   a tour   b collection
   c exhibition

12 Can you ___ life without a computer?
   a entertain   b imagine
   c try on

4 **Choose the correct answers.**

1 Emma ___ to be at the studio at six o'clock.
   a must   b might
   ĉ has

2 You ___ climb up the statue. It's dangerous.
   a mustn't   b don't have to
   c couldn't

3 'Must I watch this silly reality show?' 'Yes, you ___ !'
   a do   b must
   c mustn't

4 'Should we bring our trainers?' 'Yes, ___ .'
   a should you   b you shouldn't
   c you should

5 Wear comfortable shoes because we ___ go on a tour.
   a might   b should
   c can

6 Barbara ___ act very well when she was a child.
   a can   b should
   c could

7 This town is visited ___ thousands of people.
   a with   b from
   c by

8 Children ___ by cartoons.
   a entertain   b are entertained
   c are entertaining

9 The statue ___ every Thursday by Harry.
   a is cleaned   b be cleaned
   c is clean

10 Leonardo da Vinci ___ the helicopter, did he?
   a didn't invent   b wasn't invented
   c isn't invented

11 This series ___ for the first time in 1978.
   a shown   b was shown
   c is shown

12 Was the smartphone ___ for John?
   a bought   b be bought
   c was bought

11 From Here to There

Lesson 1

1 Write the missing letters.

1 This is the part of the road where you ride your bike. b <u>i k e</u> l <u>a n e</u>

2 This is where you arrive at the end of a journey. d _ _ _ _ _ _ _ _ _ _

3 This is a person who walks to get somewhere. p _ _ _ _ _ _ _ _ _

4 This is where you wait for the bus. b _ _ s _ _ _ _

5 This kind of car doesn't use petrol or oil. e _ _ _ _ _ _ _

2 Match.

1 traffic — d
2 get on
3 parking
4 tram
5 motorbike
6 get off
7 scooter
8 driver

76 UNIT 11

3 Choose the correct answers.

1 Martin is the _____ driver in the family.
   a good
   b better
   (c) best

2 There are _____ people at the bus stop than usual.
   a more
   b many
   c most

3 My car isn't as fast _____ yours.
   a than
   b from
   c as

4 This is the _____ journey I've ever been on.
   a more exciting
   b most exciting
   c exciting

5 Tram tickets were _____ last year than they are now.
   a cheaper
   b the cheapest
   c cheap

6 Travelling by train isn't as _____ as travelling by motorbike.
   a more tiring
   b tiring
   c most tiring

4 Look at the pictures and write T (True) or F (False).

1 The smallest bike is the fastest. F
2 The left car isn't as expensive as the middle car.
3 The caravan isn't as new as the bus.
4 The train is older than the motorbike and the car.
5 The bus is the most popular way to travel.
6 The grey plane is more dangerous than the white plane.

5 Circle the correct words.

1 Ferries are (more) / most expensive than coaches.
2 Walking to work is **better / the best** than driving.
3 What is **most / the most** popular means of transport in your town?
4 Bicycles aren't **as fast / faster** as motorbikes.
5 This caravan is prettier **than / as** the other one.
6 These tyres are the **cheaper / cheapest** in the shop.

Lesson 2

1 Complete with these words.

> billion   gallery   loudspeaker   timetable   ~~escalators~~

1 How many __escalators__ are there in this shopping centre?

2 Let's ask for a _____ for the buses.

3 My favourite art _____ is in London.

4 Can you hear the _____? It says our train is late.

5 Do you know that more than one _____ people used this underground railway last year?

2 Circle the correct words.

1 The street **(sign)** / **railway** should show us the way to the underground.

2 A map of the underground system is **displayed** / **moved** on every train.

3 Get your tickets out because the ticket **machine** / **inspector** is coming.

4 The escalators are broken. You'll have to take the **timetable** / **lift**.

5 You can buy your train tickets from that **gallery** / **machine**.

3 Find the transport-related words and use them to complete the sentences.

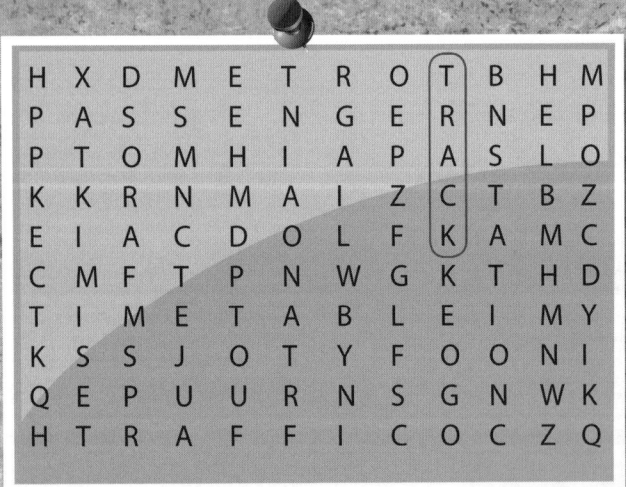

H	X	D	M	E	T	R	O	T	B	H	M
P	A	S	S	E	N	G	E	R	N	E	P
P	T	O	M	H	I	A	P	A	S	L	O
K	K	R	N	M	A	I	Z	C	T	B	Z
E	I	A	C	D	O	L	F	K	A	M	C
C	M	F	T	P	N	W	G	K	T	H	D
T	I	M	E	T	A	B	L	E	I	M	Y
K	S	S	J	O	T	Y	F	O	O	N	I
Q	E	P	U	U	R	N	S	G	N	W	K
H	T	R	A	F	F	I	C	O	C	Z	Q

1 The Glasgow underground has only got 10.4 kilometres of __track__.

2 The _____ got off the train and ran for a bus.

3 This _____ says there aren't any trains for two hours!

4 There's a lot of _____ on the road so let's take the train.

5 We'll meet at Bond Street _____ at two o'clock.

78   UNIT 11

4 Look at the train timetable and write *T* (True) or *F* (False).

From	To	Leaves at	Arrives at	Length of journey	Comments
Madrid (Atocha Station)	Seville (Santa Justa Station)	7:00	9:30	2 hours 30 minutes	runs Monday - Friday
Madrid (Atocha Station)	Barcelona (Sants Station)	7:30	10:54	3 hours 24 minutes	runs every day
Madrid (Atocha Station)	Cordoba (Central)	6:30	8:20	1 hour 50 minutes	runs Monday - Friday
Madrid (Chamartin Station)	Barcelona (Sants Station)	22:20	7:20	9 hours	runs every day

1 You can get a train to Barcelona from both Atocha Station and Chamartin Station. **T**

2 Neither of the trains to Barcelona run on a Sunday. ☐

3 You can travel to either Cordoba or Barcelona from Chamartin. ☐

4 Both trains to Barcelona leave in the morning. ☐

5 You can't arrive in either Seville or Cordoba before eight o'clock in the morning. ☐

6 Neither the journey to Seville nor the journey to Cordoba takes more than two and a half hours. ☐

5 Choose the correct answers.

1 _____ the ticket machines nor the escalators work.
   ⓐ Neither   b Either   c Both

2 You can travel either by tram _____ bus into town.
   a nor   b and   c or

3 Janice can drive _____ buses and trains.
   a neither   b both   c either

4 You can take the Underground to _____ Charing Cross or Oxford Street from this station.
   a neither   b both   c either

5 _____ the number 64 bus and the number 18 bus go past the museum.
   a Both   b Neither   c Either

6 This city has got neither trains _____ trams.
   a nor   b and   c or

6 Complete the paragraph with *both, either* or *neither*. Sometimes more than one answer is possible.

The Museum of Transport is very popular with (1) __**both**__ local people and visitors to the city. It was opened in 1954 and was built using money from a famous car maker. There are two main exhibitions in the museum. They are Land and Sea Transport and Air Transport. You can visit (2) _____ of them from 9 am to 5 pm from Monday to Friday. You can (3) _____ go on a guided tour or look at the different means of transport on your own. Unfortunately, (4) _____ exhibition is open at the weekends, but you can visit the museum on Saturday mornings and listen to an interesting talk about (5) _____ the history of transport or plans for the future. You should miss (6) _____ of these talks! They're fantastic!

Lesson 3

1 Match.

1 How much is a return   a car?
2 Where can I get a water   b station?
3 Where can I get a cable   c ticket?
4 How much is a travel   d taxi?
5 Where is the nearest metro   e pass?

2 Circle the correct words.

1 There aren't **too many / enough** tickets for everybody. We need two more.
2 This tram is going **enough / too** fast!
3 Some people have to get off the bus as there are **too many / enough** people on it.
4 She was **too / enough** tired for a walk.
5 The train crashed because the driver wasn't careful **too / enough**.
6 We can't get the tram now. It's **too late / late enough**.

3 Complete the dialogues with these questions.

SAY IT LIKE THIS!

Can I buy a single ticket to Duke Street, please?   Can I buy a travel pass, please?
Can I travel to the island by sea?   ~~Excuse me, how can I get to Hope Street?~~
Where do I get off the bus for the cinema?
Where do I get off the metro for the transport museum?

1 **Man:** Excuse me, how can I get to Hope Street?
   Woman: You can take the bus from the stop in Wellington Street.

2 **Boy:** _____
   Man: Yes. A single ticket costs £1.40.

3 **Woman:** _____
   Man: Yes. A travel pass costs £55 for one month.

4 **Girl:** _____
   Man: You get off at the next station.

5 **Man:** _____
   Woman: You can take the ferry from the harbour.

6 **Boy:** _____
   Driver: You get off at the next stop.

4 The headings in the report below are in the wrong order. Read the report and change the order of the headings.

> **Remember!**
> When you write a report, put a heading above each part. The heading should tell the reader what each part is about.

~~Timetable~~ <u>How can we get to the islands?</u>
At the moment, not many ferries come to our islands. For this reason, most people go to other islands either by water taxi or plane.

Cost _____
At the moment, you can only get to some islands either very early in the morning or late at night and this isn't easy for passengers. Also, there are no ferries at the weekends to most islands.

What can we do? _____
Another problem with our ferries is the price of tickets. The cost of return tickets is too high. For some journeys the cost of return ferry tickets is the same as the cost of a flight to the same island.

How can we get to the islands? _____
The ferries to our islands can become more popular if we change a few things. Firstly, we can change the times of ferries and make sure that some leave during the day. Also, we can have special prices for groups of people and make return tickets cheaper. I think these changes will make the ferries more popular.

5 Write a report about the problems with a means of transport in your city. Use this plan to help you.

Paragraph 1
Say what means of transport you are going to talk about and say that it could be better.

Paragraph 2
Say what one of the problems is and discuss why this is a problem.

Paragraph 3
Say what another problem is and discuss why this is a problem.

Paragraph 4
Suggest ways to deal with the problems.

81

12 Jobs

Lesson 1

1 Complete the sentences with these words.

> ~~customer~~   detective   chef   mechanic   reporter

1 Mr White is a __customer__ at my dad's shoe shop.
2 My car isn't working so I'm taking it to the _____ this afternoon.
3 The _____ is looking for clues to the kidnapping.
4 I don't know how to make ice cream; I'm not a _____ .
5 The _____ asked Liz some questions about the story.

2 Match.

1 artist **b**
2 sailor ☐
3 queue ☐
4 reporter ☐
5 chef ☐
6 detective ☐

3 Circle the correct words.

1 Water slide testers **listen / (check)** for safety.
2 Can you post your **homework / opinion** about our restaurant on social media?
3 Queue-sitters have to be very **patient / boring**.
4 My shop is very busy, we have lots of **customers / people**.
5 You need good social media **skills / companies** to work as a water-slide tester.

4 Circle the correct words.

1 The boat sailed **quick / (quickly)** down the river.

2 He can fly **high / highly** in the sky in his new plane.

3 Magda has got a **beautiful / beautifully** guitar.

4 The children ate the sandwiches **hungry / hungrily**.

5 The detective found the missing necklace **easy / easily**.

6 The **angry / angrily** taxi driver got out of his car.

5 Complete the job advert with adverbs made from the adjectives in brackets.

Chef wanted for boat

Do you love travelling, but can't afford a holiday this year? Can you cook (1) ___well___ (good) enough for the most difficult of customers? Then come and be one of the chefs on the boat *Ocean Spray*. Our chefs work (2) _____ (hard) every day. They prepare food very (3) _____ (fast) but very (4) _____ (careful). Our chefs all work (5) _____ (happy) together as a team. We give free time every day so they can lie (6) _____ (lazy) under the sun. If you enjoy sailing, you will love this job!

Give us a call now on (234) 556 7399.

6 Answer the questions.

1 What do you always do wrong? _____

2 What do you always do right? _____

3 Who can swim quickly in your family? _____

4 Who sings badly in your family? _____

5 What food do you eat noisily? _____

6 When do you not think clearly? _____

Lesson 2

1 Choose the correct answers.

1 Is your job full-time or _____?
   a) part-time
   b day off
   c Mondays

2 _____ are good at drawing and choosing colours.
   a Sailors
   b Designers
   c Managers

3 I can go to the beach tomorrow because it's my _____.
   a job
   b day off
   c career

4 My sister is an _____. She's very good at writing.
   a author
   b chef
   c actor

5 Have you got any _____ designing websites?
   a career
   b focus on
   c experience

6 Do you enjoy your _____ as a reporter?
   a career
   b employee
   c manager

2 Complete the sentences with these words.

   part-time   focuses on   job   full-time   designer

1 Some of my friends have got __part-time__ jobs. They only work at the weekends.
2 I'm starting a new _____ on Monday. I'm excited!
3 My mum is very busy. She works _____ as a reporter.
4 The project _____ using the new technology.
5 My uncle has an interesting career. He's a costume _____.

3 Circle the correct words.

Karen Hughes was a new (1) **career / employee** in a company which sells gardening equipment. She didn't have any (2) **company / experience**, but she was good at her job. One day an old man called. He wanted to speak to the (3) **staff / mechanic**, Mr Jones, because he had a machine from the company which cuts grass and it wasn't working. Karen explained that it was Mr Jones' (4) **day off / job** but the man was upset because he wanted to cut the grass for his wife's 60th birthday party in the garden. Karen felt sorry for him. She left the office and went to the man's house. She fixed the machine and even cut the man's grass. The next week, the company got more than 20 phone calls from people who were at the birthday party. They all wanted to buy the same machine. Karen's (5) **manager / remover** was very happy and he gave Karen some extra money.

Karen Hughes
Employee of the month

84 UNIT 12

4 Match.

1 This is the photographer — e who took the photograph.
2 I worked in an office
3 Angela works for a company
4 Marple is the town
5 That's the artist
6 That's the computer

a which I used to use.
b which sells cars.
c where there were no windows.
d who had an exhibition last week.
e who took the photograph.
f where I went for a job interview.

5 Complete the sentences with *who*, *which* or *where* and these phrases.

| chefs are trained | ~~work~~ | find criminals | is busy |
| live in the wild | the company opened an office | | |

1 Employees are people _____ who work _____ for others.
2 Snakes are animals _____ .
3 Heather is a woman _____ 24 hours a day.
4 Detectives are people _____ .
5 This is the school _____ .
6 This is the town _____ .

6 Put the words in the correct order to make sentences.

1 teachers / schools / people / in / who / work / are
   Teachers are people who work in schools.

2 restaurant / John / where / that's / works / the
   _____

3 Angela / which / job / she / a / really / has / enjoys / got
   _____

4 driver / had / there's / who / the / accident / the
   _____

5 which / take / work / bag / blue / the / I / to / is / one / the
   _____

6 teachers / are / where / schools / places / work
   _____

Lesson 3

1 Write the missing letters.

1. This person works in a police station.   p<u>o l i c e</u> o<u>f f i c e r</u>
2. You study here.   c _ _ _ _ _ _ _
3. It is sad when this happens to people, animals or plants.   d _ _
4. This person flies planes.   p _ _ _ _ _
5. This is where chefs work.   k _ _ _ _ _ _ _

2 Complete the dialogue with these words.

> **SAY IT LIKE THIS!**
>
> ~~explaining~~   fixing   helping   qualifications   skills   working
>
> **Brian:** Hi, Gary. How are you? You don't look very happy.
>
> **Gary:** I know. I'm alright really. But it's my parents. They're always asking me the same thing, 'What do you want to be when you grow up, Gary?'
>
> **Brian:** Well, what do you want to be?
>
> **Gary:** Oh, I don't know.
>
> **Brian:** I want to be a teacher because I'm very good at (1) __explaining__ things. I also enjoy (2) _____ people understand new ideas.
>
> **Gary:** But teachers need a lot of (3) _____ .
>
> **Brian:** I know, but I can get them at college.
>
> **Gary:** But teachers need a lot of (4) _____ too. They must be good at lots of things.
>
> **Brian:** I think I'll be a good teacher. I'm very patient and I love (5) _____ with children. Haven't you got any idea what you want to do? What are you good at?
>
> **Gary:** Well, I'm very good at (6) _____ machines, so I might become a mechanic.
>
> **Brian:** Yes, that's a good idea.

3 Talk to your partner about the job you want to do. Explain what qualifications and skills you need for this job and what is good and bad about it.

4 Read the article below and complete the notes with the main ideas from the article.

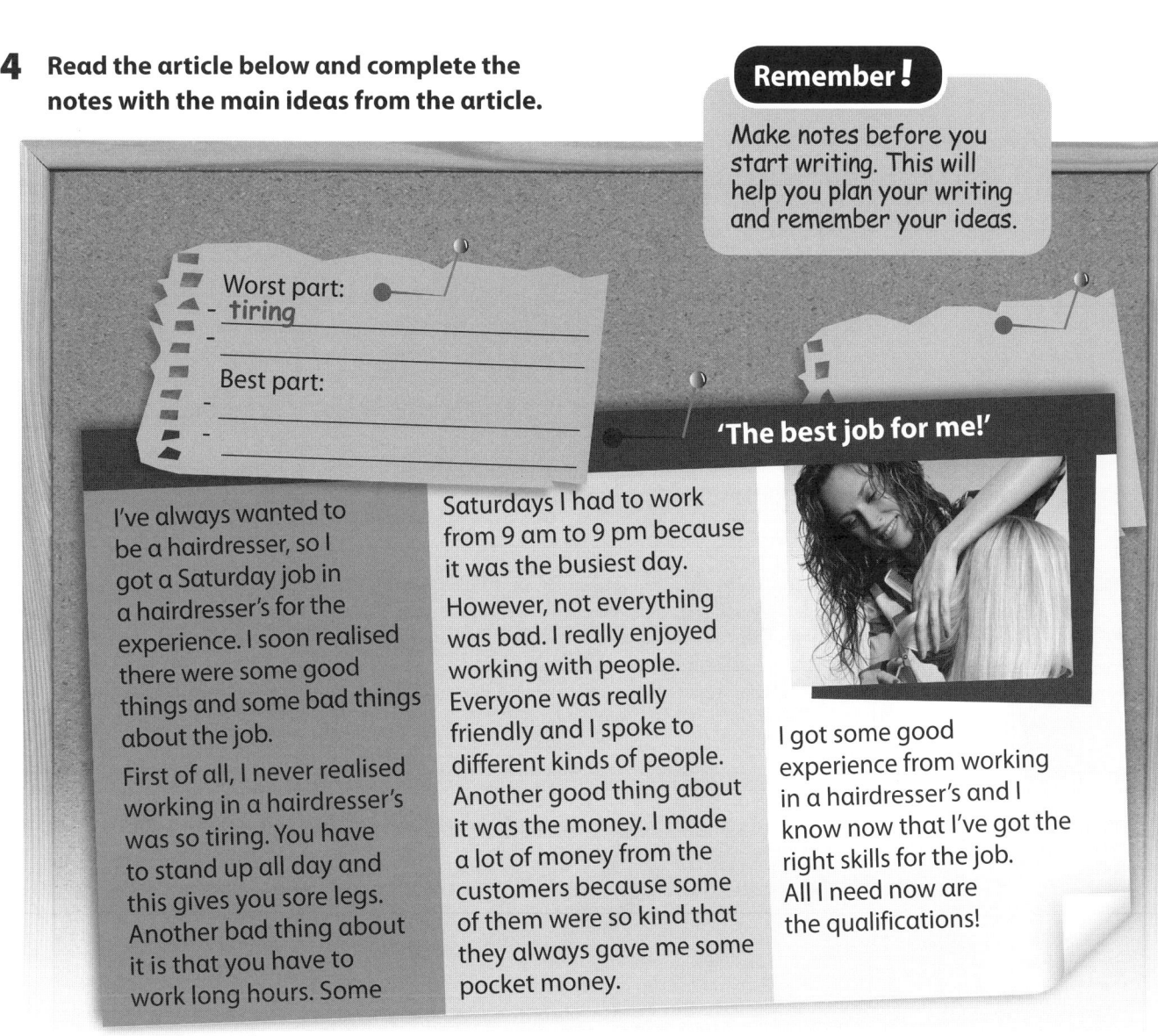

Remember!
Make notes before you start writing. This will help you plan your writing and remember your ideas.

Worst part:
- tiring
- _____
- _____

Best part:
- _____
- _____

'The best job for me!'

I've always wanted to be a hairdresser, so I got a Saturday job in a hairdresser's for the experience. I soon realised there were some good things and some bad things about the job.

First of all, I never realised working in a hairdresser's was so tiring. You have to stand up all day and this gives you sore legs. Another bad thing about it is that you have to work long hours. Some Saturdays I had to work from 9 am to 9 pm because it was the busiest day.

However, not everything was bad. I really enjoyed working with people. Everyone was really friendly and I spoke to different kinds of people. Another good thing about it was the money. I made a lot of money from the customers because some of them were so kind that they always gave me some pocket money.

I got some good experience from working in a hairdresser's and I know now that I've got the right skills for the job. All I need now are the qualifications!

5 Write an article which talks about the good and bad parts of a job. Use this plan to help you.

Paragraph 1
Introduction. Say what job you are going to write about and that there are good things and bad things about it.

Paragraph 2
Write about the bad things and explain why they are bad.

Paragraph 3
Write about the good things and explain why they are good.

Paragraph 4
Conclusion. End your article.

Review 6 — Units 11–12

1 Read the text about fruit picking.

People have always had to work. The kinds of jobs people do every day change. New jobs appear and some jobs disappear. One job which is in danger of disappearing in Britain is fruit picking.

Every summer farmers need help when they pick their fruit. Picking fruit isn't always easy, but it is a fantastic job for students who are on holiday during the summer months. They can work part-time or full-time on fruit farms. They are paid for every kilo of fruit they pick and usually they can pick about ten kilos of fruit every day. Farmers normally show workers what to do with the fruit and it takes them about a week to learn.

Nowadays, most students are not interested in doing this kind of work. They prefer working indoors in cafés or restaurants during the summer holidays. Farmers often can't find enough fruit pickers and some fruit is wasted.

If you like working outdoors, try fruit picking. It's a skill that is learnt easily and can help you make some pocket money too!

2 Write *T* (True) or *F* (False).

1. Fruit picking is a new job in Britain.   **F**
2. Farmers pick all their fruit alone. ☐
3. All pickers must work all day on fruit farms. ☐
4. Fruit pickers are paid for every hour they pick fruit. ☐
5. Fruit picking is easy to learn. ☐
6. Most students love working outdoors. ☐

3 Choose the correct answers.

1 There are a lot of ___ on the road today.
   a (buses)   b boats
   c cable cars

2 You can buy a monthly ___ pass if you want.
   a single   b return
   c travel

3 Let's take the ___ . I can't walk up the steps.
   a escalator   b timetable
   c ticket machine

4 I hate sitting in ___ .
   a stairs   b traffic
   c luggage

5 Are you working full- or part- ___ ?
   a time   b job
   c staff

6 Get off at the next ___ for Shettleston.
   a street sign   b stop
   c traffic

7 I want to get some work ___ as a designer.
   a professional   b patient
   c experience

8 Please ___ on the lesson, James!
   a focus   b get
   c display

9 This company has got 50 members of ___ .
   a employees   b managers
   c staff

10 My dad has a ___ in advertising.
   a career   b day off
   c living

11 There are five ticket ___ in this station.
   a speakers   b machines
   c galleries

12 The ___ is coming. Take out your tickets.
   a inspector   b detective
   c sailor

4 Choose the correct answers.

1 Craig is the ___ mechanic in the world!
   a bad   b (worst)
   c worse

2 Taking the bus is ___ than taking a taxi.
   a too cheap   b cheapest
   c cheaper

3 Please show me the artist's ___ paintings.
   a nicest   b most nice
   c nicer than

4 This job isn't as interesting ___ I imagined.
   a than   b as
   c then

5 The pilot went as ___ as he could.
   a high   b higher
   c highly

6 We can ___ travel by plane or ship.
   a neither   b either
   c nor

7 I can't be a detective, I haven't got the skills ___ the qualifications.
   a and   b or
   c nor

8 This cable car isn't ___ for all these people.
   a bigger   b big enough
   c big

9 The policewoman shouted ___ at the criminal.
   a angry   b angriest
   c angrily

10 This is the motorbike ___ hit me.
   a who   b what
   c which

11 They're going on a journey ___ lasts three months.
   a which   b who
   c where

12 I can't remember ___ I left the snake!
   a who   b which
   c where

89

PROJECT 1
Being Together

1 Look at the pictures and write what the people are doing.

He's playing tennis.

2 Make a list of things you like and don't like doing.

Like	Don't like
I like riding my bike.	I don't like cleaning my shoes.

3 Choose one of the things you like doing from Activity 2. Make some notes about it.

- how often
- when
- where
- with who
- equipment
- why I like it

4 Take some photos or draw a picture of you doing your activity.

5 Write a description of what you are doing in the picture(s).

1 Use the present continuous to talk about what you are doing. (For example: I'm wearing my new jacket.)

2 Use the present simple to talk about habits and routines. (For example: I usually go to the sports club every Tuesday and Thursday afternoon.)

6 Bring your picture(s) and writing to school and display them. Look at your friends' pictures and read their writing.

PROJECT 2 Where Do You Live?

1 Look at the pictures and label them.

~~a modern house~~   a flat   a houseboat   a cottage

A modern house

2 Answer the questions.

1 Which home do you like most and why?

2 Which home don't you like and why?

3 Think about your home and make some notes about it. What rooms does it have? Write *yes* or *no* and how many it has.

4 Take some photos or draw a picture of your home. Make a plan of the rooms in your home and label them.

5 Write a description of your home, its rooms and where it is in town. Use your notes from Activity 3.

6 Make a model of your dream home.

7 Bring your model to school and display it. Look at your friends' models. Which do you like best and why?

PROJECT 3 Try Something New

1 Look at the pictures of sports. Label the one with no title.

ice climbing

bungee jumping

_____

windsurfing

whitewater rafting

paragliding

2 Answer the questions. Which of these extreme sports can you do …

1 in winter? _____
2 in the air? _____
3 on water? _____

3 Which of the sports in Activity 1 do you think is the most dangerous? Why?

_____
_____
_____
_____
_____
_____

4 Work in pairs. Choose a sport and research it. Make some notes about it.

- Where do people do it?
- When do people do it?
- What equipment do you need?
- Is it very dangerous? Why / Why not?
- Other information

5 Find some photos or draw some pictures of people doing your sport.

6 Make a poster with your partner using your pictures and information.

7 Work with two other pairs who have posters about different sports. Each give a short talk on your sport.

Our extreme sport is ... We chose it because ... People do it ...

PROJECT 4

Food and Drink

1 Look at these foods from different parts of the world.

Place: China
Name: Bird's Nest Soup
How: The nests are collected and cooked in water and eaten when soft. You eat the bits of trees and plants that make the nest.

Place: South-East Asia
Name: Durian
How: You open the fruit and eat the soft part around the seeds. BUT the fruit has a terrible smell!

Place: Wales
Name: Laverbread
How: Laver is a type of seaweed. The seaweed is boiled for several hours. The paste that results is then rolled in oatmeal and fried.

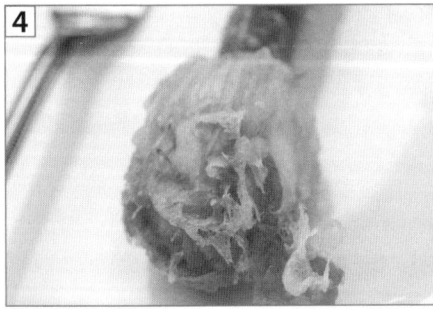

Place: Italy
Name: Fried Zucchini Flowers
How: The flowers are picked from the zucchini plants and can be stuffed with herbs and cheese and baked or deep fried.

2 Work in pairs. Do you think you would like to eat these foods? Why / Why not?

3 Work in pairs. You are going to make a meal of very strange food! Say how to prepare and eat each thing.

For example:

> **First course:** Fried Door.
> Take one door from a house and remove the paint from it. Chop it up into small pieces. Heat some oil in a pan, then fry the door quickly on both sides. Put it on a plate, and serve it with a little dried grass.

Decide on your three courses and make notes.

First course:

_____
_____
_____

Main course:

_____
_____
_____

Dessert:

_____
_____
_____

4 Draw and colour a picture of each course of your meal. Write a description of each course. Use your notes from Activity 3.

5 Work in groups of four. Tell each other about your meal and show your pictures. Whose meal is the strangest?

PROJECT 5
School and Beyond

1 Look at the pictures and label them.

classroom   computer room   ~~sports field~~   library   science lab   teacher

sports field

2 Which of the places in Activity 1 do you like best? Why?

I like the computer room in picture 4 because ...

3 Think about how schools have changed. What were schools like 50 years ago? Make some notes about the differences in the table below.

Schools then	Schools now
No computers	Computers

4 Ask your parents and grandparents what schools were like in the past. Make some notes. If they have any photographs of themselves at school, ask if you can borrow them.

5 Write a paragraph called *How Schools Have Changed*. Use your notes from Activities 3 and 4 and the example below to help you.

How Schools Have Changed

Schools are very different now. When my grandparents were at school, there weren't any computers.

Children didn't have ...

Children studied ...

They didn't study ...

6 Bring your writing and photos to school. Work in groups of four. Read each other's writing. Which things are similar and which are different?

PROJECT 6 — Our Amazing Bodies

1 Look at the pictures and label them.

> mummy   necklace   jewellery   ~~pyramids~~   dress   cat statue

1. _pyramids_
3. _____
5. _____

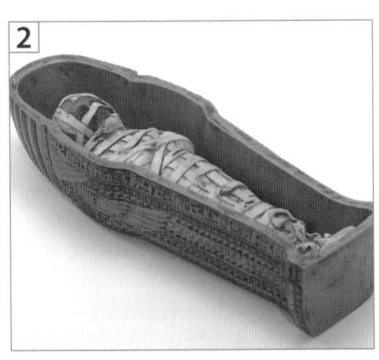

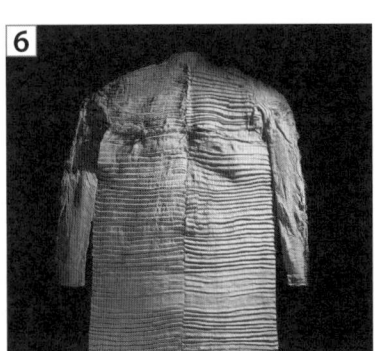

2. _____
4. _____
6. _____

2 Write some sentences describing the pictures in Activity 1. Which do you think is the most beautiful. Why?

Picture 1 is a photo of the pyramids. They are very famous. They are 5,000 years old. I think this is the most beautiful picture because …

3 Work in pairs. Find out about a particular mummy in a pyramid or tomb. Make some notes about it.

- where it was found
- when it was found
- who it is
- how old it is
- other things found with it
- other information

4 Find or draw some pictures of the mummy and the things found with it.
Write a paragraph of 75–100 words about the mummy and make a poster.

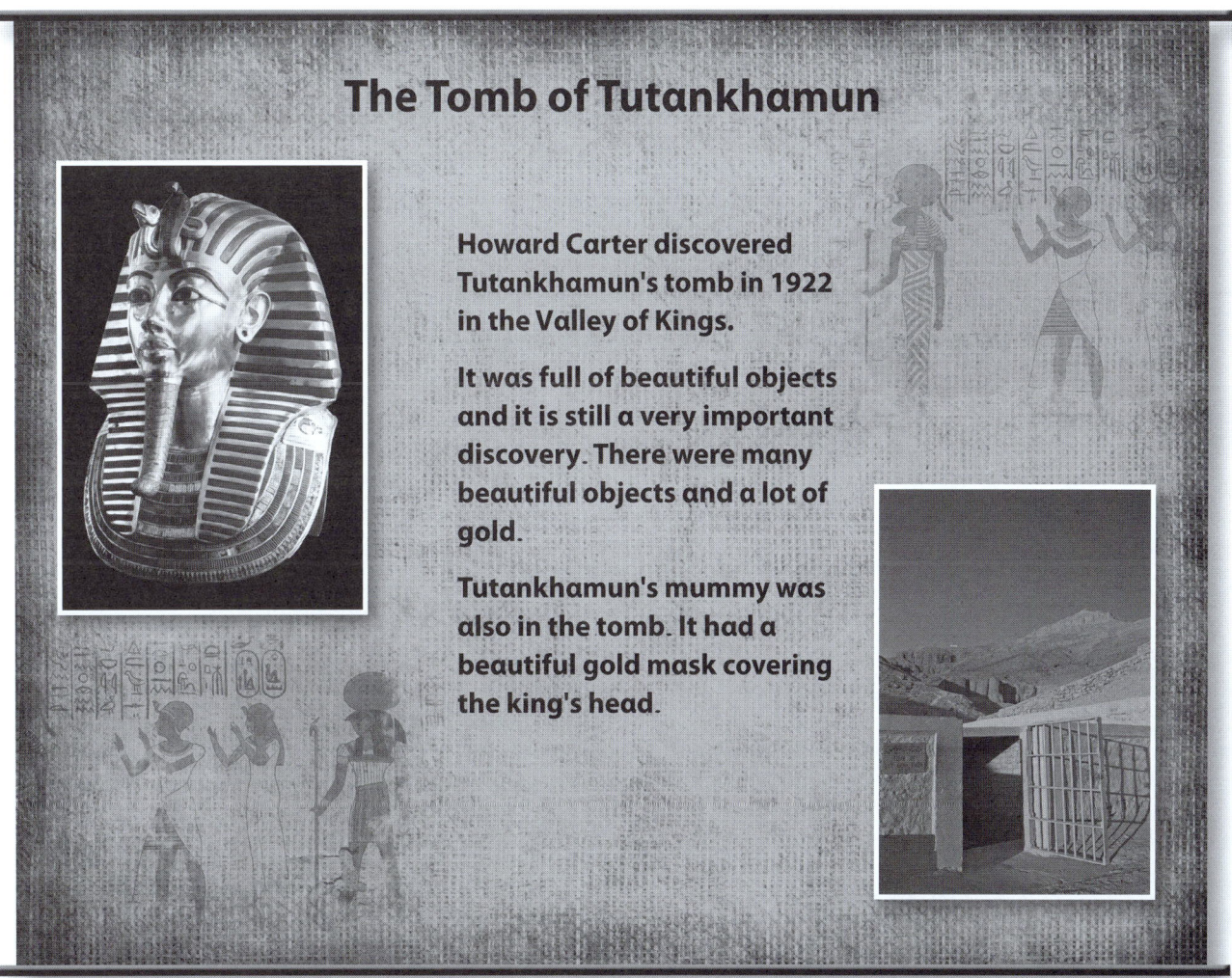

The Tomb of Tutankhamun

Howard Carter discovered Tutankhamun's tomb in 1922 in the Valley of Kings.

It was full of beautiful objects and it is still a very important discovery. There were many beautiful objects and a lot of gold.

Tutankhamun's mummy was also in the tomb. It had a beautiful gold mask covering the king's head.

5 Make a model of the tomb / pyramid your mummy was found in.

6 Display your work in class. Look at your friends' posters and models. Which do you like best? Why?

PROJECT 7 — All Around Us

1 Read the texts and look at the pictures. Write the names of the meat-eating plants.

a Venus Flytrap

The Venus Flytrap sits with its leaf open. When a fly walks on the leaf, it touches a hair that makes the top part of the leaf come down. There are long hairs along the edges of the leaves so that the fly cannot escape. Then the plant 'eats' the fly.

b Pitcher Plant

The Pitcher Plant has a sort of hanging 'cup' with a sweet liquid inside. Insects like the smell and come to see what it is. They then fall inside the 'cup' and cannot get out of the liquid. The plant then 'eats' the insect.

c Butterwort

The Butterwort has leaves that look like spoons. The leaves have lots of very small sticky balls of 'glue' all over them. When an insect walks on the leaf and gets stuck, the leaf rolls in from the sides and 'eats' it.

d Bladderwort

The Bladderwort lives under the water in lakes and ponds. It has a little bag (the 'bladder') at the end of each of its stems. When a water insect touches one of the hairs on the outside of a bag, it opens and sucks the insect inside. The insect can't escape and the plant 'eats' it.

Name: Butterwort

Name: _____

Name: _____

Name: _____

2 **Which plant do you think it the most interesting and beautiful? Why?**

<u>I think the Bladderwort is the most interesting plant because ...</u>

3 **Research one of the plants from Activity 1. Make some notes about it.**

- what countries it lives in
- the types of places it can be found
- how big it is
- what its flowers are like
- how it catches insects
- other information

4 **Find or draw some pictures of your plant.**

5 **Write a paragraph of 75–100 words about your meat-eating plant. Use your notes from Activity 3.**

6 **Use your writing and pictures to make a poster.**

7 **Bring your poster to school and display it. Look at your friends' posters. Which do you like best? Why?**

PROJECT 8
Protecting the Planet

1 Look at the pictures and label them.

> travel around the world   buy a big house   make water clean for everyone
> plant a lot of trees   ~~save money for the future~~   start a recycling company

save money for the future   _____   _____

_____   _____   _____

2 If you were very rich, which of the activities above would you do first? Why?

_____
_____
_____
_____
_____
_____

3 Imagine you suddenly have €30 million. Make some notes about what you would do with your money.

For myself: <u>Travel around the world</u>

For my family:

For my friends:

For other people:

For the environment:

Other ideas:

4 Make a poster.

1	2	3	4	5
Find a large piece of paper and draw a square in the middle, with six lines coming out from it. Draw another box at the end of each line.	In the middle box write: If I had €30 million, I would …	Label the other boxes with the headings from Activity 3.	In each of the boxes write what you would do with your money. If you want to add other boxes, you can.	Do a drawing beside each box to illustrate one of the things you have written in it.

5 Bring your poster to school and display it. Look at your friends' posters. Who has had the best ideas?

105

PROJECT 9 City Life

1 Look at the pictures and label them.

> park university café ~~hotel~~ library castle

hotel

2 Which of these places have you got in your town?

In my town, we have got a university and a … We have also got …

3 Work in pairs. Make a list of the important buildings and places in your town.
(For example: The Palace Hotel, National Bank, History Museum.)

_____

_____

_____

_____

_____

4 Draw and colour a big map of part of your town. Write the names of the main streets, buildings and places on it.

5 Bring your map to school. Give a short talk about one or two of the important buildings on your map. Include this information.
- how old it is
- who built it
- how many people visit it

This is our map of … You can see a … , a …. and a … There is also a … There isn't a … in our town.

PROJECT 10 Share and Enjoy

1 Look at the pictures and label them.

> comedy   ~~documentary~~   sports   quiz show

documentary

_____

_____

_____

2 Which of these TV programmes do you like and not like? Why?

I like watching ... and ... because ...
_____
_____
_____
_____

3 Make a timetable of the week with eight columns and eighteen rows.

Time	Sunday	Monday	Tuesday	Wednesday	Thursday	Friday	Saturday
07.00 – 08.00							
08.00 – 09.00							
09.00 – 10.00							
10.00 – 11.00							
11.00 – 12.00							
12.00 – 13.00							
13.00 – 14.00							
14.00 – 15.00							
15.00 – 16.00							
16.00 – 17.00							
17.00 – 18.00							
18.00 – 19.00							
19.00 – 20.00							
20.00 – 21.00							
21.00 – 22.00							
22.00 – 23.00							
23.00 – 24.00							

4 When you are watching TV, write in your timetable what kind of programme you watch and when. (For example: `comedy, cartoon`.)

How many hours of TV do you watch a week? _____

5 Work in groups of four. Show each other your timetables.

1 Who watches the most / the least TV? _____

2 Are there any programmes you all watch? _____

3 Are there any programmes you watch that the other three never watch? Why? _____
_____

6 Write a paragraph of 75–100 words about your week's TV viewing.

PROJECT 11 From Here to There

1 Look at the pictures and label them.

ferry   bus   tram   underground   train   taxi

bus

2 Which of these types of public transport have you used? Write about when and where.

3 Write two sentences about which type of public transport you like best and why.

I like trains best because ...

_____

4 Choose one type of public transport that operates in your town. Draw a map of the town centre. Show some of the places the transport goes to and where it stops.

5 Find some of the things in the picture and make a model of your chosen public transport.

6 Bring your model and map to school. Give a short talk. Say what is good and bad about the service you have chosen and how and when you use it.

This is my model of a ... I chose it because I like ... The ... service in my town is ...

PROJECT 12 Jobs

1 Look at the pictures and label them.

> chef   doctor   sailor   police officer   reporter   taxi driver

doctor

2 Which of the jobs in Activity 1 would you most, and least, like to do? Why?

The job I would most like to do is ... because ...

3 Which job would you like to do when you are older? Make some notes about it.

- if you have to study (if so, for how long?) _____
- indoors or outdoors _____
- how many hours a week _____
- the good things about the job _____
- the bad things about the job _____
- other information _____

4 Research your ideal job further. Make some notes about it.

5 Find or draw some pictures of someone doing the job. Write a paragraph of 75–100 words about your ideal job. Use your notes from Activities 3 and 4.

_____
_____
_____
_____
_____
_____
_____
_____

6 Stick your picture(s) and writing onto a large piece of paper and make a poster.

7 Bring your poster to school and display it. Look at your friends' posters about their ideal jobs.

Wordsearches

Unit 1
Find these words.

~~lazy~~ laugh grandchildren danger population
hurt protect frightened waste enjoy

L	A	Z	Y	N	G	E	A	A	V	I	O	L	E	A
Y	F	R	I	G	H	T	E	N	E	D	O	P	R	K
L	A	U	G	H	O	U	D	A	N	G	E	R	V	E
O	H	A	R	K	R	S	T	Z	K	T	A	R	X	W
A	U	W	X	L	W	I	T	L	A	P	T	O	L	A
G	R	A	N	D	C	H	I	L	D	R	E	N	R	S
C	T	M	L	Y	L	L	U	G	F	A	N	H	Y	T
C	L	O	V	E	R	Y	I	S	B	I	J	E	V	E
G	S	E	P	O	P	U	L	A	T	I	O	N	A	Y
P	R	O	T	E	C	T	A	Y	M	O	Y	H	T	L
C	T	S	L	Y	L	L	U	G	F	A	N	H	Y	I
O	H	A	R	K	R	S	T	Z	K	T	A	R	X	L

Unit 2
Find these words.

~~rich~~ pay armchair coffee fridge
sink window rug plastic earthquake

E	L	S	N	C	O	B	A	B	K	M	R	I	C	H
L	I	B	C	O	F	F	E	E	S	L	N	A	F	O
E	K	D	A	R	F	L	H	O	M	S	W	O	R	K
A	E	A	R	A	R	M	C	H	A	I	R	E	O	A
R	H	R	N	Y	M	I	A	C	E	N	L	A	S	S
T	I	S	I	T	O	R	S	P	A	K	E	T	I	P
H	S	G	J	W	E	R	P	S	M	L	A	U	N	L
Q	T	F	R	I	D	G	E	E	K	L	N	V	G	A
U	O	S	E	N	D	R	B	S	R	E	L	N	O	S
A	R	R	E	D	K	P	A	Y	O	C	X	S	V	T
K	Y	U	D	O	B	O	L	E	A	T	H	I	M	I
E	O	G	L	W	R	C	O	A	S	T	E	R	S	C

114 WORDSEARCHES

Unit 3

Find these words.

~~dive~~   hobby   rope   tired   relaxed
explore   sure   slide   trick   wrong

O	K	F	D	I	V	E	O	G	I	A	N	T	B	S
M	M	T	O	N	A	L	M	F	K	K	O	P	S	T
T	I	R	E	D	N	D	E	O	N	B	E	F	D	I
K	E	I	H	C	J	A	R	E	L	A	X	E	D	J
E	P	C	E	K	S	N	W	L	F	C	P	T	C	H
M	T	K	T	L	O	C	A	K	E	H	L	H	O	W
P	V	Q	B	S	C	E	I	D	L	E	O	R	A	R
L	S	U	G	U	O	V	T	M	A	E	R	O	F	O
A	L	I	S	R	O	P	E	N	N	S	E	W	C	N
Y	I	E	C	E	K	H	R	I	C	E	H	J	F	G
H	D	T	A	B	S	F	B	L	N	I	D	B	O	U
T	E	A	E	D	E	L	I	H	O	B	B	Y	B	L

Unit 4

Find these words.

~~soup~~   pot   thirsty   seafood   full
meat   boil   delicious   hang on   disgusting

S	O	U	P	O	P	H	Y	F	L	D	N	D	S	T
A	F	T	U	N	L	D	S	T	H	I	R	S	T	Y
S	D	L	N	K	K	E	T	I	A	S	I	C	K	L
T	F	U	L	L	I	L	T	L	N	G	N	T	P	S
L	R	A	E	P	C	I	R	O	G	U	S	O	C	T
E	A	U	R	S	K	C	A	T	O	S	S	R	H	F
L	I	M	E	B	D	I	I	J	N	T	F	L	A	T
O	S	E	A	F	O	O	D	R	O	I	V	A	M	B
P	R	A	C	T	I	U	E	B	S	N	U	N	P	O
U	A	T	L	F	N	S	R	O	S	G	T	N	I	S
S	F	G	I	J	P	O	S	I	M	G	S	P	O	T
H	B	C	O	A	C	H	L	L	B	O	X	I	N	G

Unit 5

Find these words.

~~break~~   canteen   strict   report   understanding
interview   advert   sweatshirt   cheat   friendship

C	O	T	B	R	E	A	K	S	L	O	I	D	S	T
A	F	T	U	N	L	C	S	W	F	A	N	O	R	K
S	D	L	N	A	K	H	T	E	H	F	T	C	K	L
T	T	E	N	D	I	E	T	A	E	O	E	T	P	S
L	R	A	E	V	C	A	R	T	S	T	R	I	C	T
E	A	U	R	E	K	T	A	S	C	P	V	R	H	F
R	E	P	O	R	T	O	I	H	R	G	I	L	A	T
O	N	W	Q	T	F	N	N	I	O	S	E	A	M	B
P	R	A	N	M	E	O	S	R	A	N	W	I	P	G
U	A	U	N	D	E	R	S	T	A	N	D	I	N	G
C	A	N	T	E	E	N	S	N	M	G	S	V	O	T
H	B	C	F	R	I	E	N	D	S	H	I	P	N	G

Unit 6

Find these words.

~~cough~~   lung   sore   stretch   ancient
elbow   injure   tattoo   mystery   thermometer

B	O	T	O	T	E	L	Y	F	L	C	O	U	G	H
A	E	T	U	H	O	N	T	R	O	L	A	A	R	K
L	L	O	C	E	K	I	T	I	H	F	R	D	K	M
C	B	W	O	R	R	S	T	L	S	O	T	D	R	Y
S	O	R	E	M	A	I	N	O	W	M	A	E	U	S
N	W	R	T	O	L	L	A	T	I	P	T	R	N	T
Y	I	V	I	M	A	N	C	I	E	N	T	O	N	E
O	N	W	N	E	X	T	N	R	M	S	O	A	I	R
P	R	A	J	T	I	R	A	C	E	R	O	N	N	Y
S	A	I	U	E	N	G	R	O	R	L	U	N	G	M
S	F	I	R	R	T	O	C	Y	C	L	I	N	G	E
S	T	R	E	T	C	H	L	G	Y	M	N	A	S	T

116 WORDSEARCHES

Unit 7

Find these words.

jungle   erupt   branch   iguana   stone
volcano   leaf   slippery   wildlife   sticky

J	U	N	G	L	E	L	Y	F	L	I	W	L	O	O
A	F	T	U	C	O	N	T	R	O	L	I	A	R	K
L	L	O	C	K	L	I	T	I	H	S	L	D	K	L
C	O	W	O	N	E	S	T	L	S	L	D	D	R	S
O	O	E	B	R	A	N	C	H	W	I	L	E	U	T
V	R	R	T	E	F	L	A	T	I	P	I	R	N	I
O	I	V	A	L	A	C	H	A	M	P	F	O	N	C
L	S	T	O	N	E	T	N	R	M	E	E	A	I	K
C	R	A	E	X	I	R	A	C	E	R	U	N	N	Y
A	A	I	L	I	N	G	R	O	R	Y	T	0	G	M
N	F	I	G	U	A	N	A	Y	C	L	I	A	G	E
O	B	C	O	A	C	H	L	G	Y	E	R	U	P	T

Unit 8

Find these words.

cover   environmental   battery   product   electronics
landfill   system   petrol   pollute   dump

C	O	V	E	R	O	P	R	L	E	O	P	A	R	D
S	L	D	O	L	I	N	L	P	R	O	D	U	C	T
B	S	A	F	I	N	D	A	H	L	B	C	A	V	E
E	L	E	C	T	R	O	N	I	C	S	B	O	P	R
W	O	R	M	D	E	M	D	O	Z	T	S	N	O	V
I	W	E	S	N	P	O	F	O	A	B	Y	P	L	E
T	Y	R	T	B	E	L	I	B	D	B	S	A	L	K
T	P	O	R	W	T	N	L	Y	U	T	T	R	U	F
B	A	T	T	E	R	Y	L	Y	M	T	E	R	T	H
A	A	S	W	A	O	L	L	S	P	O	M	O	E	A
T	F	G	K	J	L	P	E	O	A	V	F	T	S	V
S	E	N	V	I	R	O	N	M	E	N	T	A	L	Y

Unit 9

Find these words.

~~design~~   expensive   skyscraper   straight   cross
sight   ferry   shopping centre   right   directions

A	B	S	F	D	E	S	I	G	N	A	N	E	S	D
E	C	I	N	C	E	R	T	B	N	O	S	F	M	I
X	A	G	L	B	S	C	A	R	T	C	R	O	S	S
P	S	H	O	P	P	I	N	G	C	E	N	T	R	E
E	A	T	P	L	S	T	F	O	R	M	U	U	E	C
N	L	V	I	N	T	A	W	A	R	D	I	N	D	K
S	K	Y	S	C	R	A	P	E	R	C	T	O	R	S
I	T	F	S	I	A	G	E	R	J	R	C	Y	A	A
V	U	E	I	D	I	R	E	C	T	I	O	N	S	C
E	I	R	L	A	G	E	M	O	U	G	S	L	A	K
S	E	R	T	R	H	V	B	A	S	H	E	T	L	O
S	T	Y	G	E	T	R	I	M	E	T	L	F	G	H

Unit 10

Find these words.

~~print~~   comment   upload   sitcom   entertain
social media   app   cartoon   programme   technology

A	P	R	I	N	T	S	I	G	N	A	N	E	S	D
E	N	T	E	R	T	A	I	N	P	O	S	F	M	I
X	T	G	L	B	S	P	A	R	T	C	R	O	S	S
P	E	H	O	P	P	P	R	O	G	R	A	M	M	E
E	C	T	U	P	L	O	A	D	R	M	U	U	E	C
N	H	V	I	N	T	A	W	A	C	D	I	N	D	K
S	N	Y	S	C	R	A	P	E	O	C	T	S	R	S
I	O	F	S	O	C	I	A	L	M	E	D	I	A	A
V	L	E	I	D	I	R	E	C	M	I	O	T	S	C
E	O	R	L	A	G	E	M	O	E	G	S	C	A	K
S	G	R	C	A	R	T	O	O	N	H	E	O	L	O
S	Y	Y	G	E	T	R	I	M	T	T	L	M	G	H

118 WORDSEARCHES

Unit 11

Find these words.

~~destination~~   driver   inspector   display   scooter
traffic   gallery   timetable   parking   electric car

A	B	S	F	D	E	S	T	I	N	A	T	I	O	N
E	C	I	N	S	P	E	C	T	O	R	S	F	M	I
X	A	G	L	B	S	C	A	R	T	C	R	O	S	S
P	S	T	R	A	F	F	I	C	C	E	N	T	R	P
E	A	I	S	L	S	T	F	O	R	M	U	U	E	A
N	L	M	C	N	T	A	G	A	L	L	E	R	Y	R
S	K	E	O	C	D	A	P	E	R	C	T	O	R	K
I	T	T	O	I	R	G	E	R	J	R	C	Y	A	I
V	U	A	T	D	I	S	P	L	A	Y	O	N	S	N
E	I	B	E	A	V	E	M	O	U	G	S	L	A	G
S	E	L	R	R	E	V	B	A	S	H	E	T	L	O
E	L	E	C	T	R	I	C	C	A	R	L	F	G	H

Unit 12

Find these words.

~~mechanic~~   sailor   author   manager   focus on
opinion   detective   career   skill   artist

A	B	S	F	D	E	S	M	E	C	H	A	N	I	C
M	A	N	A	G	E	R	C	T	O	R	S	F	M	I
X	A	G	L	F	O	C	U	S	O	N	R	O	S	S
P	S	T	R	A	F	F	I	C	P	E	N	T	R	P
D	E	T	E	C	T	I	V	E	I	M	U	U	E	A
N	L	M	C	N	T	C	G	A	N	S	K	I	L	L
S	A	I	L	O	R	A	P	E	I	C	T	A	R	K
I	U	T	O	I	R	R	E	R	O	R	C	R	A	I
V	T	A	T	D	I	E	P	L	N	Y	O	T	S	N
E	H	B	E	A	V	E	M	O	U	G	S	I	A	G
S	O	L	R	R	E	R	B	A	S	H	E	S	L	O
E	R	E	C	T	R	I	C	C	A	R	L	T	G	H

Drawing page